T0209840

RELATIONSHIPS:
From DARKNESS *to*
LIGHT

A Biblical View of How Men and Women Interact

LINDSY REBEC VAIPHEI BRADY

WESTBOW
PRESS°
A DIVISION OF THOMAS NELSON
& ZONDERVAN

WestBow Press books may be ordered through booksellers or by contacting:

WestBow Press
A Division of Thomas Nelson & Zondervan
1663 Liberty Drive
Bloomington, IN 47403
www.westbowpress.com
1 (866) 928-1240

Because of the dynamic nature of the Internet, any web addresses or links contained in this book may have changed since publication and may no longer be valid. The views expressed in this work are solely those of the author and do not necessarily reflect the views of the publisher, and the publisher hereby disclaims any responsibility for them.

This book is a work of non-fiction. Unless otherwise noted, the author and the publisher make no explicit guarantees as to the accuracy of the information contained in this book and in some cases, names of people and places have been altered to protect their privacy.

Any people depicted in stock imagery provided by Getty Images are models, and such images are being used for illustrative purposes only.
Certain stock imagery © Getty Images.

Scripture quotations marked AMP are taken from the Amplified® Bible, Copyright © 2015 by The Lockman Foundation. Used by permission.

Scripture quotations marked GNT are taken from the Good News Translation® (Today's English Version, Second Edition). Copyright © 1992 American Bible Society. All rights reserved.

Scripture quotations marked KJV are taken from the King James Version of the Bible.

Scripture quotations marked NIV are taken from The Holy Bible, New International Version®, NIV® Copyright © 1973, 1978, 1984, 2011 by Biblica, Inc.® Used by permission. All rights reserved worldwide.

Scripture quotations marked NKJV are taken from the New King James Version®. Copyright © 1982 by Thomas Nelson. Used by permission. All rights reserved.

Scripture quotations marked NLT are taken from the Holy Bible, New Living Translation, Copyright © 1996, 2004, 2015 by Tyndale House Foundation. Used by permission of Tyndale House Publishers, Inc., Carol Stream, Illinois 60188. All rights reserved.

ISBN: 978-1-9736-5067-6 (sc)
ISBN: 978-1-9736-5069-0 (hc)
ISBN: 978-1-9736-5068-3 (e)

Library of Congress Control Number: 2019900337

Print information available on the last page.

WestBow Press rev. date: 01/15/2019

In loving memory of my mom and dad,
the late Mr. and Mrs. Thangpi and Ngainu Vaiphei

Following are my parents' favorite verses:

Blessed is the man Who walks not in the counsel of the ungodly, Nor stands in the path of sinners, Nor sits in the seat of the scornful; But his delight is in the law of the Lord, And in His law he meditates day and night. He shall be like a tree Planted by the rivers of water, That brings forth its fruit in its season, Whose leaf also shall not wither; And whatever he does shall prosper.

—Psalm 1:1–3 (NKJV)

I have no greater joy than to hear that my children walk in truth.

—3 John 1:4 (NKJV)

I love you, Mom and Dad.
Your loving daughter,
Lindsy Rebec Vaiphei Brady

Contents

Preface

This book comes together from my experiences in the natural and as well as supernatural realms of the body, soul, and spirit. It took me many years to put this book together from what I learned and experienced and from what God revealed to me. Since the beginning of my life, I have always sought to gain knowledge and wisdom about life and understand how it works. As I have traveled through life, I have had many questions because of my lack of understanding. I believe there are so many people who question life just as I have done, wanting to know reality and to seek the kinds of answers that I have sought.

At a very young age, the bad experiences I had, including the trauma I went through because of my parents, family, and friends and because of the surroundings I grew up within, put a big question in my head: Why? I especially wondered about relationships, which I continued seeking to understand for many years. Going through pain and oppression and facing various difficult situations made it hard to cope. I couldn't understand anything back then, and there was no one I could ask. The people around me had their own struggles, with questions of their own. Being a Christian doesn't give one all the answers. I was born and brought up in a Christian home, but nothing was clear until God touched me and revealed it to me. I came to know that clarity is not about Christianity; it is about having a personal relationship with Him.

God is so gracious and so full of mercy and love. When I sought after Him wholeheartedly, from those broken and dark places, He rescued, healed, and restored me. He establishes me in His word when I seek Him daily with prayer and fervent cries. I seek Him with all my heart, mind, soul, and strength. He has provided for me and given me the strength, through His Spirit, to understand my world and myself. He gave me the strength to forgive myself, my past, and those who hurt and who oppressed me. He blessed me with a beautiful, faithful, and humble husband who accepts me the way I am and who supports and stands by me. My husband has helped me put this book together so that I can express my experiences and the wisdom I have learned. My hope is to help others who face darkness and bring them to light.

God also has revealed many things beyond measure to me while I've been learning about the meaning of human life. I want to share this wisdom and help others discover who they really are and how unique and precious every individual's life is. It doesn't matter where you stand right now. Whether you are a Christian or a non-Christian, you always can make a difference by choosing the right way.

Without complete understanding, it's easy to blame others—parents, family, friends. It's also easy to blame circumstances. It's easy to point out others' shortcomings but hard to see our own. I used to blame others, God, and myself, because I was blind and deaf in spirit and didn't know what the truth was. Until I sought after God, I was a victim of Satan and obeyed him along with what the world offered me. Examining myself in God helps me understand all I face in life, who I am, and how weak and strong I am. It helps me build myself up in God from the very foundation He gave me through Christ Jesus.

In today's world, people's minds develop according to the nature of the world. They build upon a worldly foundation and upon broken relationships, living without knowing the full answers. Even though this modern world may be changing, the pain and hurt never changes. Pain is the same yesterday, today, and forever. It tears up so many lives, breaks apart families, and even takes away many lives prematurely. I've seen and faced such pain; it is so real, and nothing can heal it without Christ. Satan uses people minds by twisting them, turning them, and later condemning them, all without taking any responsibility. If anyone is lacking in wisdom and understanding, that is where Satan takes advantage. He tempts and later binds them without any hope, but there is always hope which is in Christ Jesus.

Some are oppressed so much that they find it hard to grasp the lives they have and are still living within the bondage of guilt and shame. They may believe in God but still live under that shadow of the past. It's time to see things from God's perspective and not our own. God gave us the way to overcome the past and live in the present moment of our lives with total *freedom*. What Satan uses to destroy me turns into good; God uses it in developing my life the way He wants me to be. I thank God for those bad experiences in my past because I know who Satan is, and I know now how to fight against him. I have no fear of him. Wherever I go, he flees (the light shines and darkness flees) because of the power given me by my Almighty Father in heaven through Christ Jesus, my Savior.

I wrote this book to tell people that there is hope, there is victory, and there is life in the Spirit. There is an answer to every question, and you can enjoy everyday life with peace, joy, and completeness. Satan is a liar, a twisted serpent who is the father of all lies, and he will not stop chasing everyone to try to pull us down and bring us to destruction. But God gives us the power and authority in our hands to fight against every demonic stronghold through Christ Jesus. If we don't know that power personally, we become powerless and defeated. The power is already here on earth and is based in "knowing and understanding the knowledge of God and wisdom of truth. So let us fight the good fight of faith, in truth, to overcome all lies, for "the Lord is near to all who call upon Him, to all who call upon Him in truth" (Psalm 145:18 NKJV).

Like the book of Acts, God chose me, "To open people eyes, and to turn them from darkness to light, and from the power of Satan unto God, that they may receive forgiveness of sins, and inheritance among them which are sanctified by faith that is in me." (Acts 26:18 KJV)

And I rested in God like Psalm said, "I have set the Lord always before me: because he is at my right hand, I shall not be moved. Therefore my heart is glad, and my glory rejoiceth: my flesh also shall rest in hope." (Psalms 16:8-9 KJV)

I love You, my God, my Redeemer!

Acknowledgments

Without God and my husband, I would not have been able to complete this book. My husband stood beside me, helping me through each step. Thank you, my love, for your obedience to God and for your faith in me. Your love has been my strength and shield during every battle. I will forever be indebted and thankful to you and to God our Father, His Son, and His Holy Spirit.

God has given me revelation upon revelation since the beginning of my life, and He guided me along the way to complete this book. It was difficult to put it together since I had never written a book before, but I really wanted to help others, especially those who had suffered as I did. It was really challenging at times, and I almost gave up, but God said to me, "It is not your will nor your power but My will and My power." I knew right then that God wanted me to continue. With my faith in Him, I believed in my heart that this book would touch and restore millions of lives to give them hope, wisdom, and understanding and to set them free from every bondage. God really has strengthened me from inside and out.

I also thank God for placing such wonderful people in my life to help me, stand with me, encourage me, and stretch out their hands to bring me to where I am today. I would like to thank my family in Christ in India, Pastor Kanchan and her family for their help and support. My Aunt Rhonda, who sacrificed her life by coming over to India for my wedding; she faced many difficulties but patiently waited for my blessing to come. Even though she may no longer be here on earth, her legacy of blessings that she left me will continue to bless others. I thank First Assembly of God Brookhaven, Pastor Jim and Kim Mannon, and all their church members who supported my husband and me during our difficult moments. They provided my beautiful wedding gown and helped me come to this beautiful country from India. Also, I would like to thank Mr. and Mrs. Ed and Debbie Crawford and their family for their friendship, time, love, support, and effort. I especially would like to thank Debbie Crawford for her sacrifice. She took the initiative and labored to arrange our beautiful wedding shower. I cannot thank her enough for her patience, love, dedication, and effort.

I thank Pastor Joey and Patricia Pedreira from Bride Adorned Church in Slidell, Louisiana. for their love and support when they opened the church for us to renew our vows and celebrate a wonderful day in our lives. I would like to thank Spring of Praise World Outreach Center in Crystal Spring, especially Pastor Darrell Blankenship and his wife for allowing my husband and me to step into ministering to those who were in need and helping me in my transitional period. I thank Pastor Otis and Twila Lichlyter for their support and love. I thank Pastor Larry Wilson for his word of truth and for helping my husband and me by allowing us to be the people God wants us to be.

I thank my mother-in-law and father-in-law, Betty and Larry Brady, and my sister and brother-in-law, Cherie and Freddie Calcote, for their love and support. I thank my sweet friend Rachel Russell and her family for their love and friendship as well; Rachel is my angel whom God sent to me to cheer me up when I was alone. I also thank Sister Naomi Boyte and Sister Yvonne Gable, who loved me and comforted me during my most difficult moment, when my mom passed away (4th March 2015). They both are really a great blessing to me, and I know I can lean on their shoulders anytime. I thank Sister Nancy Gilpin, who loves me and encourages me and who took precious time helping me with editing this book.

Without you all, I could not be where I am today. I give thanks from the depths of my heart. I may not be able to bless everyone accordingly, but I have prayed that God, whose love is abundant, will bless you all a hundredfold for all the good deeds you have done for my husband and me.

I thank my mom and dad for what they taught me, showed me, and let me experience. They both suffered tremendously and sacrificed until the end to keep the family together in Christ. They may not have had an earthly treasure to leave me, but they left me a great treasure, wisdom and knowledge, which will last forever.

Above all, I thank God, who has blessed me with His promises, has given me an understanding heart, and has blessed me abundantly. I would not be where I am today without Him. He is my refuge, my shield, and my everything. Praise and honor unto Him forever!

1

Men and Women Knowing and Understanding the Self: Foundations

God has made from one blood every nation of men (all races) to dwell on all the face of the earth and has determined their preappointed times and the boundaries of their dwellings, so that they should seek the Lord, in the hope that they might grope for Him and find Him, though He is not far from each one of us.

—Acts 17:26–27 (NKJV)

Men and Women: Differences and Responsibilities

God created men and women according to His image. He gave both men and women unique foundations for operations on earth. Their God-given responsibilities are to complete each other and to fulfill what God calls them to be for His pleasure.

What do you think are the distinctive characteristics and natures of men and women?

I believe you already have seen some of the differences as well as the similarities. Both are equal in God's eyes, but they were created differently and for different purposes. They are different in physical appearance, but inside their hearts and souls are no differences. Their behavioral and character differences are because each was developed according to the way they were trained. Let's look at the foundations of men and women through their differences and their responsibilities in God.

Foundations of Men and Women:
The Masculine and Feminine Sides of God

In Genesis, God created man in His own image and likeness—that is, in the masculine side of God. Man looks like God (the Father), which means man is another form of God. This means men can function according to the nature and character of God, acting and behaving like God, and they are able to think and speak like God. Even though he is not equal with God, man was created to be like Him. This is the same as a child who looks like his father, which everyone can understand, because the child has the same genes of the father, but the child doesn't understand fully what the father's heart is until the child becomes mature enough to understand a father's position. God created man—who has the same genes as God—and put him on earth to rule and govern, to have dominion and power upon and above the earth.

The foundation of men was to rule and govern with power and dominion, according to God's instructions. This is a very strong character for men to have. This is the masculine side of God.

The Bible says, "Now out of the ground the Lord God had formed every beast of the field and every bird of the heavens and brought them to the man to see what he would call them. And whatever the man called every living creature, that was its name" (Genesis 2:19 NKJV).

God trained and allowed Adam to operate in His dominion and power, as manhood is not inborn but must be achieved. In many cultures, boys endure painful initiation rituals to become men. It's about training. God trained Adam to be a man. He trained Adam to govern and to rule by giving him a task and placing responsibility on his shoulders. This task is given to all men, from one generation to another.

The task is to exercise and train man to be man, to operate in power, authority, and to have dominion over the earth. In the beginning, God also gave Adam the highest gift a person can have—"a solid relationship with Him." He shared and communicated with Adam directly. God's male character—the masculine side—operates in power and authority, which means there's no backing down from what He says. Yes means yes, and no means no. Whatever Adam called every living creature, that was the creature's name. Adam was created to work and conquer, to be tough and strong, to achieve, to provide, and to fulfill demanding tasks. It's really kind of hard and harsh, but that is the very character and nature of man, according to what God wants him to be.

When a man works and conquers—gains control and governs—it's like a piece of cake on his plate that satisfies his soul and spirit. Even today, men love to have power, authority, and dominion in one way or another. No one can change this nature except for God, by His spirit. So many women in today's world try to change men according to their own desires, but most of them fail. Men haven't forgotten what has been given to them since the beginning. They fight against one another to take back what has been lost since Adam's fall. That is why, from what you see, read, and hear from the history of the world, men have repeatedly tried to take back what was lost, claim their own territories, and rule and govern where they can. It's in their blood.

The foundation of women was to help; women reveal the softer side of God. God created women in His image—same genes—as helpers and supporters for men. Who will be a good companion to men, and who will strengthen them inside and out? Women have different natures and characters, unlike men. When you see women (the helpers), you can see the sensitive, compassionate, and affectionate side of God. Helpers have the characteristics of willingness, humbleness, patience, kindness, goodness, gentleness, and long-suffering, which can be summed up as love. This reflects the Holy Spirit speaking through Jesus in the book of John: "And I will pray the Father, and He will give you another Helper, that He may abide with you forever" (John 14:16 NKJV).

Where women are lacking in being true helpers, the Holy Spirit fills in the lack. The Holy Spirit has the complete characteristic of being a perfect helper: the Spirit is calm, peaceful, patient, wise, gentle, kind, full of grace, compassionate, loving, and forgiving.

Weaknesses of Men and Women

Adam did not recognize where he was in life. He did not realize that it was not good to be alone. It was God who knew where he stood. Also, in the Bible, we can see how God visited him in the cool of the day. These visits were not about Adam seeking the Lord; it is God who visited him.

I can see how Adam enjoyed the garden of Eden: swimming in his own world and playing with nature, animals, and birds. He didn't bother much with his relationship with God because he knew, in the back of his mind, God was with him. On the other hand, we can see how much God longed to have a good relationship with Adam (because of God's feminine character). But men have the tendency to enjoy their own worlds and do their own things without wanting to be disturbed or controlled. In this also lies great weakness. When a woman longs to have a good relationship with her man, this is her weakness. Meanwhile, the man is enjoying his own games, away from any relationship, knowing in the back of his mind that she is there for him, as he did to God. Men think that if they provide what is needed, they have completed all their responsibilities. That means that they really don't know the feminine side of God.

According to the Bible, "The Lord God said, 'It is not good for the man to be alone. I will make a helper suitable for him'" (Genesis 2:18 NIV). God created woman. He created her specifically to help man out and to wake him up to let him know that there is a God who wants to connect with him. God gave woman as a helper to man; she was taken out from his side—the soft, feminine, and compassionate side of God—to comfort Adam inside and out and to help him understand the soft side of God. Likewise women were to see and understand the masculine side of God through men. But women didn't understand the true meaning of the word *helper*, according to God. Eve helped her man fall into sin and death. A helper can help others to salvation or help them fall into condemnation.

In another way, men's weaknesses are that outwardly they are not very sensitive, compassionate, or affectionate. They don't show their emotional sides, whereas women long to have companions who are compassionate, affectionate, and loving, because that's who they are. Generally, men are visibly stronger outwardly and weaker inwardly, while women are stronger inwardly but weaker outwardly. One can see that men hardly cry, considering crying to be too feminine for them, but that doesn't mean they never cry. They are fighters with the strength to conquer and to achieve, but inside they still have soft hearts.

In this world, many men and women don't get the proper godly training. They grow up in environments where they make choices according to the nature of the weakening world. Women can express their masculine traits and behaviors, depending on the upbringing and training they get, just as men can express their feminine traits. Masculinity or femininity is not necessarily related to a woman's or man's sexuality; sexuality is a feeling coming from one's thoughts and heart. Sexuality is a vague or irrational belief. Feeling is very deceptive. It can change at any time, like a twisted serpent. That is why so many don't know who they are—because their minds and hearts are twisted without God's guidance. They believe and behave according to the world's evil nature. This is especially true when they don't have God's solid foundation to stand on. They become their own biggest enemies.

For those who obey the twisted words coming from their evil hearts and minds,

But God shows his anger from heaven against all sinful, wicked people who suppress the truth by their wickedness. They know the truth about God because he has made it obvious to them. For ever since the world was created, people have seen the earth and sky. Through everything God made, they can clearly see his invisible qualities—his eternal power and divine nature. So they have no excuse for not knowing God. Yes, they knew God, but they wouldn't worship him as God or even give him thanks. And they began to think up foolish ideas of what God was like. As a result, their minds became dark and confused. Claiming to be wise, they instead became utter fools. (1:18–22 NLT)

One of my very good friends, who grew up with two sisters, learned femininity from his sisters and became one of them. Later he realized and learned how to be a man again. When men learn masculinity from God, their hearts rejoice because that's what God wants them to be. Nothing is too hard for a willing heart that repents and allows God to transform it according to His instructions. Therefore, "Renew your heart and mind daily in the Lord," so that you will not fall into Satan's traps by obeying your flesh-centered mind instead of fulfilling what God called you to be.

The Fall

Before humankind's fall, Adam was living in God's presence. He was surrounded by God's wisdom and knowledge. According to the Bible, Adam never sought after God. He just lived in God's present glory, possibly without understanding who he was in God. If he understood, he may have asked God before he took the fruit from Eve. He would have had the fear of the Lord.

When God brought the woman to Adam, he was very pleased to see his kind. His heart was comforted—though it doesn't take much for a man to be comforted. When he said, "Bone of my bones, and flesh of my flesh," he expressed outwardly his gratitude that he felt so complete. But Eve, on the other hand, was not satisfied with who she was or what she already had been given, which means she was not pleased with her status. Even though she held an elevated position as a helper, a companion (in oneness) of Adam's, she desired more. Adam was more pleased than Eve was; she forgot who she was in God!

Eve's opinionated character easily deceived her, because she didn't ask Adam before she ate the fruit. She stepped out and took the decision into her own hands, failing to show respect toward her husband. She didn't represent her marriage status when she was alone; she lived as if she were single and accepted the offer easily. This was adultery in that she accepted a different voice in order to fulfill her own pleasure. Instead of respecting her marital status by asking Adam what he thought about the offer, she made her own decision.

When a person doesn't understand where he or she stands, the person becomes weak in knowing who he or she is in God. That is where Satan took advantage of them with his twisting half-truth, stealing their identities. The serpent said to Eve, "You shall be like gods, knowing good and evil." Eve didn't know she was already like God—she didn't know her identity—and fell to temptations. She also saw the tree was good for food (which was her greediness and gluttony at work) and that it was pleasant to the eyes (which was her lust for pleasures). To Eve, it was desirable to make oneself wise (which is ambitious and selfish and means being dissatisfied with what one has). Women have the tendency to become weak and easily convinced from what they see and hear from outside sources. Also, when a woman comes to know everything about her man (his weakness or strength), it is easy for the woman to step out, taking ownership, controlling, and making decisions without consulting the husband or God. Then the disrespect comes. She unknowingly forgets her main purpose, which is to encourage, strengthen, and correctly help her man—meaning, she must respect him.

This is the same as a man not asking God before making a decision, the same as Adam not asking God before he ate the fruit. They both "disrespect[ed] the head which is Christ," and they both failed.

Curses

People sometimes do not remember their foundations and forget who they are in God. Women's opinionated characters lead their men to sin and death. Due to men being disrespectful toward God and His commandments, men put the whole world under a curse of darkness. Satan applies the same temptation today, running after women to pull down men because he knows women are easier to deceive and that they are a great weapon for bringing down men, the sons of God. Men, on the other hand, are mostly disrespectful and unaccountable to God, disobeying His commandments by running after things that don't profit them spiritually, such as money, women, fame, and power.

For women, God clearly tells them to be submissive and show respect for their men. This is a biblical commandment, because God knows women can bring their men back to God using their submissive hearts. The Bible says, "For the first man didn't come from woman, but the first woman came from man. And man was not made for woman, but woman was made for man" (1 Corinthians 11:8–9 NLT). It also says, "For Adam was formed first, then Eve. And Adam was not the one deceived; it was the woman who was deceived and became a sinner" (1 Timothy 2:13–14 NIV).

Eve disrespected Adam instead of correctly helping him; she brought him to sin and death—a spiritual death, a disconnection from God. Adam lost the most important gift—his relationship with God. It was really the darkest moment for Adam and Eve. They both suffered when the door of curses was opened upon the earth. Adam's disobedience created more damage, because the law was given to him, not Eve. He didn't fulfill his responsibility of fearing the Lord when he failed to show his spouse the fear of the Lord. The worst thing Adam did was that he didn't take any responsibility for his actions. Instead, he blamed Eve. Eve did the same. She never considered it to be her fault, instead blaming the snake. The snake, on the other hand, never handed the fruit to her; it was she who believed the unknown voice of the serpent, plucked the fruit, ate some of it, and then gave the rest to Adam. Imagine if men and women took responsibility for their sins, humbled themselves, and surrendered all at the feet of Jesus. The world would be a better place to live in.

Even today, Satan whispers, human beings tend to believe him, and so we pluck the fruit and eat it. How many people pluck the fruits of wickedness, evil, and lies; eat them; and bring curses upon themselves and their families? Then they later blame it on others. Adam and Eve sold their soul with just one fruit, and Esau with just one morsel of stew sold out his birthright. What about you? Are you going to sell yourself just to fulfill your own sexual lust, greed, self-gain, self-righteousness, and lies?

Because of his selfish desire to please the woman he loves, Adam did whatever he could to make her happy. He obeyed her blindly, without any thought of consulting God. He was deceived and lost all that God had given him, which was power, authority, and dominion over the earth. Instead, they were placed these gifts in the hands of Satan. Now all people are cursed, living in fear and shame. God cursed women by greatly multiplying the pain of bringing forth a child. A woman's desire shall be for her husband, and he shall rule over her. She will no more take the headship, being opinionated and disrespectful to him. And because of Adam, the ground became cursed, and men have been cursed to toil with hard labor all the days of their lives, from generation to generation. It is sad to consider the causes of disobedience and the consequences of sin.

Reconciliation with the Father through Christ

God's love didn't change with the conditions or situations of humankind. He didn't change His ways according to the misconduct of human beings. His love never changes. He still loves us no matter what. Even though Adam and Eve committed adultery and divorced God, God is looking forward to reconciling with all of humankind—all descendants of Adam and Eve—and marrying them again. This can happen only through faith, only by dying with Jesus on the cross and becoming born again in Him with the resurrection power. We will become new creations that God can connect again through marriage.

God's heart has always been with all His creations, and He wants to save and heal all from curses. He wants to forgive their sins, to give them new life from death, and to bring them back to light by pulling them out from darkness. He wants to regenerate and make them into new creations through Jesus Christ, who suffered and died for all: "For Christ died for sins once and for all, a good man on behalf of sinners, to lead you to God. He was put to death physically, but made alive spiritually" (1 Peter 3:18 GNB).

The world was under the curse of darkness until Jesus, the light of the world, came to save us all. The way and the life with God, which was broken by Adam, is now renewed through our Lord Jesus Christ, who is the truth, the way, and the life. No one comes to the Father but through Him. Through Jesus, we can all walk again with God, taking back what was lost and governing with righteousness and the fear of the Lord. The first Adam failed and brought death, but the second Adam (Jesus Christ) brings life and freedom. The first helper (Eve) failed, but the second helper (the Holy Spirit) teaches and guides us in all the right ways. He will never fail us. Whoever believes in Him, obeys Him, and follows Him will not walk in darkness anymore.

There is one thing Satan couldn't take away, which is *faith*. Even when he tempted Adam and Eve and took away their dominion and power and broke their relationship with God, the one thing that Satan missed was faith. Satan couldn't destroy human faith, and through their human faith, God was able to lead them into righteousness. By faith, righteousness is restored in a person. When He called out to Abraham, who walked with faith, Abraham was made righteous. But God wants us not only to walk with our faith but to walk with His Spirit so that we will have the power to fight against the enemy. God's earliest promises came true when He sent His Son Jesus Christ to die for all. Then the Holy Spirit was given to us after He ascended. Because of the Father's love, reconciliation comes through Christ Jesus, and the power of God has been restored to earth—from darkness to light—by the Holy Spirit.

God loves you no matter where you stand. It's not about what's in your past. He is ready to give you a new chapter in your life. He doesn't want you to live in the past. He wants you to live in His presence with total freedom through your faith in Him. If you believe, accept, and want to have changes in your life, then take responsibility for yourself, be humble, and confess your sins. Lie down at the feet of Jesus in full surrender. He will give you His promises, as He said, "Come unto Me, all ye that labor and are heavy laden, and I will give you rest. Take My yoke upon you, and learn of Me; for I am meek and lowly in heart: and ye shall find rest unto your souls. For My yoke is easy, and My burden is light" (Matthew 11:28–30 NKJV).

Without Christ Jesus, there is no perfect relationship on earth. He also will reveal greater things through His Spirit that you never knew before, and your life will be full of excitement, with a heart full of joy that is covered in peace. In this book, we are going to discover the true lifecycle between *God*, *you*, and your *spouse*. We will discover the true relationship, from darkness to light.

Self-Understanding from the Two Foundations: Self-Examination

> Examine and test yourselves in faith.
> —2 Corinthians 13:5 (NKJV)

It is easy to examine others, but sometimes it's hard to examine ourselves clearly. God wants everyone, especially those of us who are in Him, to examine ourselves in His word so that each of us will be able to become strong in Him and to fight the good fight of faith without wavering. This way, we can become mature in Spirit, taking back what was lost. This way, we can stand on ground that is firm and strong, to rule and govern with power and dominion. This power was given to humankind at the beginning of creation. It is more important for each of us to know and understand in faith where we stand (upon which foundation) than it is for others to know this about us. Some believe in God but do not have a relationship with Him. Some have a relationship with Him but don't know how to walk with Him.

Let's find out about the two foundations.

The First Foundation: The Foundation of the World

You're born with a foundation of the world, which is where you develop many characteristics and traits. Most things are instilled in you already by blood, through Adam, and are developed and more deeply embedded by your family, friends, and surroundings. Your understandings come from the knowledge you developed while growing up. This happened in response to what you were taught, what you saw, and what you heard.

Your body, mind, and heart have developed according to the environment you grew up in. Choices you make come from that knowledge and understanding that you have gained over the course of your life. Our own understanding is limited and is brief. In the beginning of everyone's life, before we come to know Christ, we begin to develop characters and natures from what we have learned, what we have seen, and what we have absorbed from the world. This absorption mostly develops the desire of the flesh, whereas one's choices build upon this worldly foundation to fulfill the flesh.

In a relationship, a husband and wife will react according to their own ways, saying, "This is the way I am, the way I grew up, the way I believe, and no one can change it." God finds it funny when He sees human stubbornness, boasting, pride, and ego. When a person lives from his or her worldly foundation, which he or she builds up from the beginning of life, it can put friction within that person's relationship, which leads to misunderstandings and fights. The choices everyone makes from the beginning of their lives are selfish and greedy until they learn that life is not only about their own worlds.

Look at little children; look at how much attention they seek from their parents and how much expectation they put on others for their own gain. This has been human nature from the beginning of each baby's life until each becomes born again in Christ as a new creation with new genes. David says in Psalms, "For I was born a sinner—yes, from the moment my mother conceived me" (Psalm 51:5 NLT).

This foundation is not necessarily just for non-believers or non-Christians. A Christian can still stand on this foundation while carrying the name of the Lord and unknowingly considering himself or herself a good believer. Such Christians are easily led by their mindsets and emotions and not by the Spirit. They believe they are good, which they may not. So, until they have spiritual breakthroughs, the eyes of the spirit inside of them are blind. Our spiritual eyes start off blind—inactive, dead—when we are born, because of Adam. This worldly foundation operates in the very nature of the flesh and soul and can be full of turmoil, chaos, disorder, and confusion, because evil is present in human beings themselves.

The Second Foundation: The Foundation of God through Jesus

The foundation of God through Jesus is from Christ, the solid rock. It will never break nor move; it stands forever. Anyone who accepts Christ as his or her Savior and dies/crucify with Him on the cross with repentance through obedience and submission is also raised with Him with His resurrection power. Without self-sacrifice—giving the self to die on the cross—there is no resurrection life within oneself. With self-sacrifice, the first self, who is dead, becomes born again and awakens into new life in Christ Jesus, complete with new DNA. Such individuals can feel the changes inside and out, thanks to their circumcised hearts. Such people are born onto His foundation, which was laid down by our Lord Jesus Christ, who is the hope of glory. This message is not just about believing in Jesus; it is about having a new heart and a new mind in Him.

The Bible says, "Therefore, this is what the Sovereign Lord says: 'Look! I am placing a foundation stone in Jerusalem, a firm and tested stone. It is a precious cornerstone that is safe to build on. Whoever believes need never be shaken" (Isaiah 28:16 NLT). For no one can lay any foundation other than the one we already have—Jesus Christ.

The Bible also says, "Those who are born again in Christ Jesus, they become a new creation, behold the old life is gone; a new life has begun!" (2 Corinthian 5:17). There is newness in Christ Jesus that replaces our old worldly characters and natures.

A new person born in Christ means is born upon the solid rock, the very foundation of God. Behold that the old foundation, the foundation of the world, passes away, and the new foundation begins. Now, for those who are born again, it is time to build a new building in Christ Jesus according to His instruction and His way. It is time to build up to have the very character and nature of Christ. Your old natures, desires, and wants need to change to the desires of Christ and be clothed with the newness of Christ. You must be completely transformed along the journey of life in Him; transformation is not one time thing, and neither is baptism in the Holy Spirit. Paul says to die daily is to transform and to be baptized—to have a new mindset daily according to the Spirit.

As the Bible says, "Now we have received, not the spirit of the world, but the spirit which is of God; that we might know the things that are freely given to us of God. Which things also we speak, not in the words which man's wisdom teacheth, but which the Holy Ghost teacheth; comparing spiritual things with spiritual" (1 Corinthians 2:12–13 KJV).

Walk in the Spirit so that you will not fulfill the desire of the flesh. The enemy, Satan, plans every possible way to pull you down by using your own thoughts and beliefs, so from this foundation, start working and building up without wavering. God will bring you to a complete understanding in due time. Believers encounter problems and if they stop building before they come into the fullness of God—before they complete their transformation. They mix with the ways of the world, and their minds become toxic to themselves and others. They leave their faith and become their own enemies.

Self-understanding is totally different before and after we enter into relationships with Christ. Before, we may have been able to understand ourselves outwardly. But after, through Him, we can have clearer understandings, inwardly and outwardly, by His Spirit. And we will know what steps to take and what decisions to make according to His word. Remember: just knowing Jesus is not enough to know Him completely. It is like joining the military for the first time: when you join you feel lost, because you don't know what others want you to be until you learn, listen, follow, and obey their instructions.

Walk step-by-step as a friend with Him to discover more and more of who He is, who you are, and what He created you to be. He will build you up to be just like Him. You will become Christlike; be patient.

Perceiving the Self and Freedom of Choice

How do you perceive where you stand presently?

Perception doesn't come by itself. As we said earlier, you need the Holy

Spirit to help you open your eyes to see, your ears to hear, and your heart to perceive. Self-understanding means understanding the deep motives behind anything you do or say. When self-understanding comes to you in words or in deeds, ask if it is the truth, according to God, or if it is emerging from selfish motives.

Now examine yourself to see which foundation you stand on today. If you are still on the world's foundation, it is time to move to the spiritual foundation. Break through to the next level. It's time to examine yourself in Spirit to know and understand completely the stage you stand upon so that you will not be disqualified. Put yourself to the test and judge yourself so that you can find out whether you are living in faith. Surely you know that Christ Jesus is in you? Therefore, run not with uncertainty, and fight not as one who beats the air. Discipline your body and bring it into subjection, unless you should become disqualified. The Bible says, "Blessed are those whose lawless deeds are forgiven, and whose sins are covered; Blessed is the man to whom the Lord shall not impute sin" (Romans 4:7–8 NKJV).

God is Spirit, and we need to live in Spirit so that we will be able to understand all things in Him. Satan will not take you for granted anymore, as he did Adam and Eve. You can stand on your feet with the help of the Holy Spirit. You can have a clear heart and mind and complete understanding. You can fight the good fight of faith and receive all the blessings that God has kept for you. It's in your hand: *take it.*

God gives everyone the freedom of choice, so you need to be wise in choosing the right foundation.

Have you found this solid rock in your life? If not, search for Him with all your heart. When you search Him with all your heart, you will find Him as He promised. If you already found Him, continue seeking Him, for He has so many spiritual things to reveal to you. His guidance and instructions are never ending. He speaks to those who relate to Him. Not only that, but He will also bless, protect, and comfort those who walk with Him. He loves to impartially give all He promises.

Being born again, you can differentiate by the Spirit whether something comes from the self or from God, for the Spirit judges spiritually. What man knows the things of man, except for the spirit of man, which is in him? Even so, no one knows the things of God except the Spirit of God.

So if someone is not from the Spirit of God, how can that person know the things of God? How can that person be so sure that what he or she does comes from the Lord? A carnal man receives things carnally, and a spiritual man receives things spiritually. We have received God's Spirit, not the world's spirit, so we can know the wonderful things God has freely given us.

Your own spirit knows who you are, what you did, and what are doing. It is by self-examining with God's word and by hearing what His Spirit says that you will be able to recognize yourself more clearly, because the word of God is a reflection—a mirror in which you can look at yourself. However you absorb and perceive the truth, the Holy Spirit will help you. Don't read the word of God for others; read for yourself to see and understand God's perspective, and you will come to know where you stand.

The Word of God, a Mirror, and a Liquid living Word

The word of God is a mirror that reflects an individual's life in order to let an individual see where he or she stands. It is also a liquid living word that can penetrate and even divide soul and spirit, joints and marrow; it judges the thoughts and attitudes of the heart. It brings out all dirt, debris, and uncleanliness from inside our minds and hearts. God speaks in two ways: the written word and the word from the Holy Spirit.

Have you ever examined yourself with the word of God to see what your relationship with Him looks like? How often do you hear His voice? Do you obey His voice when He speaks to you? Do you know how precious and special your life is in God? There are more questions you can ask about yourself through the word of God in order to have a better understanding of yourself, which makes life clearer.

A lot of people know others better than they know themselves. Self-understanding plays a very important role in each of our lives, whether to build up or to tear down our relationships and ourselves. Discovering your foundation enables you to know where you stand and who you really are. Without discovering that foundation, it is hard to build up lasting relationships with others. This is the place where people are lost and where people blame themselves, others, or even the situations and circumstances they are going through. The level of self-understanding differs from person to person, as does how others view us.

One time I believed I was quite genuine in what I said until my husband told me I was quite negative most of the time. I realized he was right. I repented and asked forgiveness from God, and I sought God's help to blot out all negative thoughts within me. I didn't realize this about myself until he told me. My negativity was because of my upbringing and my previous surroundings. I learned and adopted it and lived with it, until God helped take it away from me. It was within me, embedded in me. I myself didn't know what I had until it was highlighted under the light.

Knowing the self is good for your body, soul, and spirit. It is also going to help you shape your life the way it was originally intended to be. It will help you with self-control, knowing justice, and knowing truth, which will make you wiser, clearer, and happier in your decision-making. But if you don't have God or the Spirit of God, you are not standing on the foundation of God, and your understanding will be very dull and most likely confused. If you know and have accepted Christ as your Savior, but it seems you are standing in the same place with no change, then you had better seek Him. That is a dangerous situation to be in, because stagnant water is a breeding ground for bacteria, mold, and parasites that can be harmful to your health and to others' health.

There are so many Christians stuck in the same place and same situation, and they can't understand why. It is because they stopped eating spiritual food (the word), they stopped seeking quality time with God, and they stopped growing in Him by listening to Him. Be truthful and honest about yourself in God. Admit if you are wrong, and embrace what is true. Otherwise, you will become stagnant, and no new things will come into your life. Stagnant Christians are not healthy Christians; they have become sick and contaminated. The foundation of the Spirit gives clarity to the mind: "For God hath not given us the spirit of fear; but of power, and of love, and of a sound mind" (2 Timothy 1:7 KJV). It is healthy to live and walk with the Holy Spirit. So speak the *truth* and walk and live in *truth* in order to live a healthy and fruitful life.

Desires and Wants: Dreams

I am sure you've had visions, dreams, or desires in your life about your relationship. You have likely dreamed about and envisioned details about your life and the future and your relationship. Your life's conditions and circumstances don't stop you from dreaming and envisioning what your life could be. Those who have bigger desires find that just thinking about those desires brings excitement and enthusiasm. As they say, some people really desire the American dream. Many do whatever it takes to achieve their dreams, while others are already having their dreams come true and are enjoying them to the fullest. We are going to discuss the reality of dreams that come from the body, soul, and spirit.

No matter how big a person's desire and how much he or she has achieved, each of us faces reality during the good times and during the worst times. The difficulties and challenges in life differ from one person to the next. Some have had worse moments of life, such as living with a major wound that they can't fix. Meanwhile, others are at the peak of enjoying life, such as in a relationship. No matter where you stand, God is the healer and the provider. There is nothing difficult for Him, especially for those who believe and obey.

There are three places where desires and wants come from:

- the flesh
- the soul
- the spirit

These three parts form the foundation of human life. It is very important to understand how each part works, because all of these play a huge role in shaping up or tearing down your life as well as the lives of others around you.

You might be familiar with these three categories. Understanding them will give you the unobstructed vision to differentiate between which one is right and which one is wrong. It will also help you make the right decision so you can enjoy life to the fullest, which God wants for each of us. Human beings have so many different backgrounds and personalities.

But with respect in how God created us, we're the same. God created human beings in three parts: the body, the soul, and the spirit.

The Body: Desires and Wants from the Flesh

The body is first operated through its five senses: sight, hearing, taste, smell, and touch. These connect the body with things of the material world. The body is the most outward and visible part of our being, and it operates in the physical realm. All physical desires and wants come from these five outward senses, and we pursue them out of a desire to feel good. The spark comes from something you see or a word you hear, which makes you excited. The touch you feel and the taste you get from what you experience and the smell that can awaken you—all of this comes from the flesh. The body is sensual, meaning it is involved in gratifying the senses for physical pleasure.

> ➤ Physical pleasures for human beings include
> - wealth—money or other material richness
> - power—obtaining worldly things whenever desired
> - ambition—achieving worldly dreams
> - fame—being famous, leading an ambitious life
> - beauty—making oneself appealing in order to lust for pleasure

All the above pleasures need a lot of labor and are challenging. They are expensive and require extreme amounts of money. That is why a lot of people fall into loving money so much that they bring greediness and selfishness into their lives. God warns everyone very clearly not to love money, because it is the root of all evil. When a man achieves things from bodily desires, such as those mentioned above, people call him wise and powerful on earth, but God may not see him that way. The book of James says, "This wisdom does not descend from above, but is earthly, sensual, demonic. For where envy and self-seeking exist, confusion and every evil thing are there" (James 3:15–16 NKJV).

According to Psalms, "We are merely moving shadows, and all our busy rushing ends in nothing. We heap up wealth, not knowing who will spend it" (Psalm 39:6 NLT).

Proverbs also teaches, "When hooked on greediness, a person struggles to get out of greed's trap. It's the same with any addiction, such as pornography, which is a manifestation of the lust of the eyes and the flesh: people become trapped. It's like the Bible says: Hell and Destruction are never full; So, the eyes of man are never satisfied" (Proverbs 27:20 NKJV).

I understand people might be wondering why God didn't allow anyone to have all possible wealth, power, or ambition. The way of God is mysterious, and He doesn't operate according to humankind's perspective. He is not a boring God. He provides more good things than what human beings expect, because when we search according to the way of the world, our search adds sorrow to ourselves and others. But when God provides, He adds no sorrow. He will provide all you need in life with peace, joy, and satisfaction. Also, you will know the God who provides, and you will give all glory to Him. For God wants all things to be according to His glory, as all things come from Him—great and small. God's ability gave Moses his fame when he stood in front of Pharaoh. God gave him the power he had when he brought Israel out from slavery, and Moses humbled himself under the mighty hands of God. It was the same with Jesus in the book of Philippians, "Who, being in very nature of God, did not consider equality with God something to be used to His own advantage; rather, He made Himself nothing by taking the very nature of a servant, being made in human likeness. And being found in appearance as a man, He humbled Himself by becoming obedient to death–even death on the cross!" (Philippians 2:6–8 NIV)

The sin of the flesh is so obvious, and the flesh will not inherit the kingdom of God. So, as the Bible says, "you must put to death, then, the earthly desires at work in you, such as sexual immorality, indecency, lust, evil passions, and greed (for greed is a form of idolatry). Because of such things God's anger will come upon those who do not obey Him" (Colossians 3:5–6 GNB). The flesh is weak. Just as you presented your members as slaves of uncleanness and of lawlessness, you will lead them to more lawlessness, which adds up to more sin. Sin after sin causes more blindness and brings you to eventual senselessness. That much sin has the power to darken all understanding and will lead to a complete loss of all sensitivity. Sins give themselves over to sensuality and indulge in every kind of impurity. Sins walk full of greed.

So present your members as slaves of righteousness for holiness. For when you were slaves of sin, you were free from righteousness. But when you are slaves to righteousness, you are free from sin. The Bible says, "What fruit had ye then in those things whereof ye are now ashamed? for the end of those things is death." (Romans 6:21 KJV)

Money

So many people poison themselves with money. They say money is the answer to everything, but it is also very deceiving, for money can't buy salvation or peace. Does money have power? Yes, but the power of money can destroy oneself quickly, and when a person is drawn into that power, his or her life becomes miserable, for the rich, according to Ecclesiastes, "have so much that they stay awake worrying" (Ecclesiastes 5:12 GNB). This takes away peace. The Bible also says, "Whoever loves money never has enough; whoever loves wealth is never satisfied with their income. This too is meaningless." (Ecclesiastes 5:10 NIV).

Money is powerful, but God is much more powerful. God is the only answer you will ever need. Money can destroy the body and soul, but God can destroy all, including the human spirit. So be fearful of the one who can destroy all. It is good to labor, earn money, and have money with righteousness. It is good to enjoy the reward of your blessings with loved ones. There is so much involved in reaching the worldly dreams that enabled one to achieve that money, though. Not only labor is required. There is a lot more involved that comes from the dark, secret world that binds people unhealthily and dreadfully for life.

What are your desires and wants on this earth? Do you fall into this area that was just mentioned?

A lot of people are hooked on fulfilling fleshly pleasure, and they go forward to get all of this by moving from one person to another, but they are never satisfied. It is very addictive if there is no control. Self-control is from the fruit of the Holy Spirit. Without God and His Spirit, many people manipulate one another by behaving like people they are not and fooling one another. If they are not careful and don't know the truth, they will become victims of brokenness.

It is easy to be caught up in outward appearances and put our desires and wants in them. Walking with this kind of desire is tiresome and will wear you down quickly, because your mindset will never be a place of rest. You will always be fighting your thoughts and dreams about how to get what the flesh wants. You will build up your expectations as you calculate how you can have achieved what you desire.

People from all walks of life have wishes for their lives. When they see something beautiful and captivating, they start desiring to possess it like Eve; this is a natural feeling of want. If there is not much self-control, this want can expand beyond measure until it becomes a huge problem in life—an example of this would be a hoarding disorder. This disorder can hinder your life and relationships. It can become greedy, and greed is the root cause of many problems. Greed is an idol that the Lord hates. When your expectations are high but the result is not what you wanted, this will lead you to great disappointment. This is where your mindset starts controlling your emotions until you easily become negative and resentful.

God wants us to be in order and rich—rich in Him and in the richness He gives. He adds no sorrow to the riches he gives us. His richness is very different from what the world offers.

God wants everyone to be blessed abundantly, above all richness and power. The way of God's richness is different from the way of the world. He doesn't want you to put your trust in money and richness; He wants you to trust in Him and put your hope in Him. James says, "Come now, you who say, 'Today or tomorrow we will go to such and such a city, spend a year there, buy and sell, and make a profit'; whereas you do not know what will happen tomorrow. For what is your life? It is even a vapor that appears for a little time and then vanishes away" (James 4:13–14 NKJV).

True Happiness and Joy

We all love to be recognized for who we are and for what we accomplish in life. It is good to be honored for every achievement. It is good to have goals, dreams, and visions that will help us in our focus and help us reach the destinations of our dreams. Finding true happiness or true satisfaction is what most people seek in life. The challenging work they put in, the money they earn, and the things they achieve—whether getting married or becoming famous, rich, or popular—are all because of happiness. They search and search to find true happiness or true satisfaction, but they may not find it as abundantly as they expect to, because they search in the wrong way. In the end, this pursuit can bring death, as Proverbs says: "There are ways which seemeth right unto a man, but the end thereof are the ways of death" (Proverbs 16:25 NKJV).

Happiness is possible only if a person's circumstances are pleasing. One does not have happiness while sick or in prison. Joy, on the other hand, is a fruit of the Spirit of God. Joy is a deeply settled peace and sense of well-being. The saint has deep joy that flourishes in good times and bad, when at liberty or in prison, when in good health or sick, and when prospects are good or dreadful. The further we walk with the Lord, the stronger and more consistent our joy becomes.

As is written in the Bible, "The Lord said that He gives us of His joy. These things have I spoken unto you, that my joy might remain in you, and that your joy might be full" (John 15:11 KJV).

Happiness is of the flesh. Joy is of the Lord. The kingdom of God is righteousness, peace, and joy in the Holy Spirit of God. I've encountered several people's problems with why something went wrong and how it happened. I've seen them fighting so hard to get what they wanted in life, but even when they achieved it, their happiness hasn't lasted long. The very thing they run after becomes a burden to them. They carry it day and night, and they don't know how to get rid of it. People might have all kinds of richness, fame, and desire, but they can still live miserable lives internally. The way of short-term happiness (also known as *shortcut richness*) is always deceptive and can easily become addictive. Satan uses this tool to tempt everyone, including Jesus. You can see a lot of celebrities who have earthly wealth, fame, and fortune but still feel empty deep inside. In this fast-paced world, their expectations are quite high for their jobs, families, and spouses or partners—and each of these things can be quite demanding of them as well. This is when people start taking drugs or alcohol to numb the pain inside.

As is written in Ecclesiastes, "Everything is wearisome beyond description. No matter how much we see, we are never satisfied. No matter how much we hear, we are not content. History merely repeats itself. It has all been done before. Nothing under the sun is truly new. Sometimes people say, 'Here is something new!' But actually, it is old; nothing is ever truly new. We don't remember what happened in the past, and in future generations, no one will remember what we are doing now" (Ecclesiastes 1:8–11 NLT).

There is a place inside everyone where God reigns, and until God occupies that place, people feel empty, shallow, and void. They may find happiness in many things, but it will not bring them into perfect joy. Joys come from within and only from the Holy Spirit. If anyone doesn't fill himself or herself with the love of Christ, his or her life becomes lonely.

It is good to see both sides of life. Look at your high expectations: when your expectations aren't met, how do you feel? You already know your world is shaking and will touch your soul, which may produce anger, resentment, condemnation, fault finding, and so on. This is selfishness. It is putting the *self* in self-righteousness. When this happens, your mindset may go into self-pity and might start rolling into blaming others or even blaming God. This happens because you believed a twisted and selfish word coming from the mind to try to fulfill the desire of the body. The body and the soul work hand in hand.

Know that, as is written in Ecclesiastes, "Here is what I have seen: It is good and fitting for one to eat and drink, and to enjoy the good of all his labor in which he toils under the sun all the days of his life which God gives him; for it is his heritage. As for every man to whom God has given riches and wealth, and given him power to eat of it, to receive his heritage and rejoice in his labor—this is the gift of God" (Ecclesiastes 5:18–19 NKJV). But in so many cases, people are obsessive, which brings disorders into the body and mind. There is just too much junk inside. When this junk is increased, attracting all creepy and crawling things, it will eventually disturb the body's system and will not be able to function properly. Fulfilling bodily desire brings short-term happiness outwardly, while inwardly there can be long-term suffering if that fulfillment of desire was used for self-gratification.

The Bible says, "Those who are in the realm of the flesh cannot please God, For when we were in the realm of the flesh, the sinful passions aroused by the law were at work in us, so that we bore fruit for death" (Romans 7:5 NIV). And as is written in Ecclesiastes, "Enjoy what you have rather than desiring what you don't have. Just dreaming about nice things is meaningless—like chasing the wind" (Ecclesiastes 6:9 NLT).

The Soul: Desires and Wants From the Soul

Soul or psyche (Greek: "psyche," of "*psychein*," meaning "to breathe") is the mental ability of a living being: reasoning and thinking, the heart's character, feeling, consciousness, memory, perception, and so on. Simply put, the soul is the mind, heart, character, and nature of a person. The Bible says, "And the Lord God formed man of the dust of the ground, and breathed into his nostrils the breath of life; and man became a living soul" (Genesis 2:7 KJV). Soul comes from the very nature of humankind; the life within people is called the self.

The soul is operated in a place unseen, but it is just as real as the body. Because of your soul, you have experienced things in the psychological realm that are mental, emotional, intellectual, interior, nonphysical, abstract, and conceptual. It is mental concepts, thinking, and reasoning that control the entire body. Controlling one's heart and emotions define a person's character and nature. The soul's desire comes from the heart and mind. The word of God says that every issue of life springs from the heart, and it says to "guard your heart diligently" because the soul holds a very strong power to tear down or to build up.

Finding love is also called finding your soul mate, a person who completes the soul. Since Adam and Eve fell, the souls of humankind have been broken, our hearts longing because of God's apparent absence. Neither men nor women can fulfill each other's internal needs completely, as both are blind to their identities in God. Women's expectations come from men, and men's expectations come from women. They both easily hurt each other. The soul is very sensitive: it can feel lonely, sad, happy, and many other emotions. If the body is sick and the soul is willing, you can still continue doing things to fulfill the will, but when the soul is sick, this really causes a problem. This is when a lot of relationships break or suffer—when the soul is not satisfied. Then Satan whispers into the mind to bring destruction that aims to destroy oneself and others.

Are your desires in line with fulfilling your soul's needs? Are you looking for someone to fill your broken soul? Are you looking for someone to fill your lonely path or to return your romantic feelings? There are many questions you can ask about finding a soul mate, whether that longing for a mate comes from the body or the soul. The soul can be weak. It can be happy or become sad in an instant, which is why a lot of people get mixed emotions, become confused easily, and make wrong choices that they regret.

The dreams and desires young people bring to relationships are mostly based on feelings, and these feelings don't last long. They can change suddenly based on what the young people see and hear, which is why the mind becomes twisted. When a romantic decision is based on emotions that have faded, confusion follows. The soul can be very deceptive and can kill the spirit instantly. Most of the things coming out of the heart and mind are too greedy and selfish, which is why a person needs to filter and clean their hearts and minds through the word of God. Even what you hear from others needs to be filtered through the word of God so you can see the truth. This psychological realm is so strong that it can control your entire body. It's like a driver for the body—a driver who takes you wherever your mind says to go. If the Spirit doesn't overpower these realms, you will be driven crazy.

The mind is what Satan uses. He twists your mind to tempt you to do something that is not right and to cause you to let your emotions control you. When your emotions control you, you become your own worst enemy because you are controlled by self, or so-called "self-love," which is selfishness. This self-pity can bring you down easily to the path of destruction. It can even poison those who are around you. The mouth speaks venomous negativity from the heart and causes destruction if unchecked. It is good to guard your heart by the help of the Holy Spirit. Cry out to God with prayer and fasting and speak in spiritual language to edify your soul, for "he who speaks in tongue edifies himself" (1 Corinthians 14:4 NKJV).

The Bible also says, "The mind governed by the flesh is death, but the mind governed by the Spirit is life and peace. The mind governed by the flesh is hostile to God; it does not submit to God's law, nor can it do so" (Romans 8:6–7 NIV).

The strongest enemy you are going to fight is yourself—your own mind. Seek the Lord, and let your mind and heart be renewed continuously. Let the Holy Spirit help you fight against your enemy. The Holy Spirit will give you power and strength to overpower and to overcome. Do not depend on your own strength and your own way. Even though you know what is right, ask for God's help, and He will direct your path. It is not about knowing; it is about understanding the perspective of God.

The Spirit: Desires and Wants from the Spirit

The third place desires and wants come from, the spirit, lies in the deepest inward part of yourself. By connecting with God spiritually, your spirit can contact the spiritual realm and know the things of the Spirit of God (supernatural things). This enables you to see the reality of life clearly. You will not only know the truth but the wholesome truth of God. You will be able to understand the heart and desire of God, and you will find it easy to obey Him. When anyone lives in Spirit and in truth, that person comes to know that he or she is not the same self anymore. What the individual wants or desires or dreams or envisions matters much less than God's will and His way.

To obtain spiritual awakening, you need to have a spiritual breakthrough. (A breakthrough is not a onetime thing.) It can happen when you seek God wholeheartedly with humbleness and full submission. As it is written, "While Jesus was here on earth, he offered prayers and supplications, with strong crying and tears, to the one who could rescue him from death. And God heard his prayers because He was humble and devoted" (Hebrews 5:7 NKJV).

Only those who are baptized in the Holy Spirit will be able to hear clearly what the Spirit says in the church. This is where God wants each person to be sanctified and purified for Him by His grace; He wants to have a perfect relationship with you. You can communicate with God directly in His Spirit, where you will be able to have revelation upon revelation to understand His wisdom. Those revelations come from God's power and will give you strength to be obedient and do the right things. Obedience to God's voice is the path of sanctification and purification in Him. Spiritual desires and wants differ from the body's and the soul's needs and wants. Spiritual desire is selfless, humble, patient, truthful, and faithful. It is not sensual, demonic, or worldly. It is pure, clean, and peaceful. It doesn't seek for the self's benefit; it seeks out the desire of the Father. Believe that you can hear the Holy Spirit, and the Holy Spirit will give you strength and power to understand.

Living in this place is called resting in God, which will bring you to the perfect life, full of joy, peace, and satisfaction. Living in the Spirit will help you operate your spiritual gifts accordingly to your walk in life. You will be able to understand deeply God's righteousness and love, which will help your heart make the right decisions. All desires from the Spirit counteract the desires from the body and soul. This is why Paul says, "For the flesh lusts against the Spirit, and the Spirit against the flesh; and these are contrary to one another, so that you do not do the things that you wish."(Galatians 5:17 NKJV) But the spirit renews the body and soul by the word of God daily, which gives us the power to fight the enemy. So, walk in the Spirit, and you shall not fulfill the lust of the flesh.

2 Meeting People: Choices

How to Understand People and Choose the Right Friends or Partner: Freedom of Choice

Are you still searching for your partner, or are you already happily married, or are you still fighting to understand people? Have you already been in a broken relationship, and if so, do you still struggle with relationships you pursue in the hope of finding the right partner?

Let us look at what God wants you to do.

The greatest gift God has given humankind is freedom of choice. God shows how much He loves us by putting no limits on human freedom of choice. We all have the freedom to change, produce, and invent. God not only gives us choices but also guidance and instructions. Even in the Garden of Eden, God gave Adam freedom of choice with instruction in what would happen if Adam didn't obey.

Some still struggle and cannot understand. They wonder how to choose the right person in life, as so many end up in regret or in painful broken relationships. This can be due to their wrong choices. These wrong choices may not necessarily result from their desires, though; these wrong choices can result from individuals' life conditions and circumstances.

Out of thousands of eligible singles just waiting for a swipe right, how do you know which person is the right one for you?

Trick question! *There isn't a right one.*

Early in life, it is easy to be blindsided by someone whom you like. It is easy to miss the most important things you should know about. Later, this can bring you some serious regret. It is good to educate oneself before any major problem happens. Even if you are already in the wrong place, you still have the power in your hand to make it right. People who are relatively uneducated (no understanding) have a higher divorce rate than ever, and when they are married, their marriages tend not to be as satisfying. The word of God says, "My people are destroyed for lack of knowledge" (Hosea 4:6 NKJV). Knowledge coming from the world is not enough; we must know the truth coming from God, which will set you free.

Being in a relationship means being connected. Connection shouldn't come because you can get something out of it; connection should come from truth and honesty and respect and love. Being ambitious to find a person who will meet your needs will bring strife, because it is selfish. Do not build a relationship based on feelings; feelings go away easily. A marriage relationship is two imperfect people joining hands and deciding to help each other in good and bad times to meet God's desires. So, how will you make the right decision despite all the situations or circumstances you may face?

Knowing People

You will meet a lot of people in life through friends, social gatherings, events, and organizations. Everyone has his or her own unique nature and behavior. As discussed earlier, all are shaped by how they grew up, what they see, and what they learn. Because we have been born with sin and iniquity since Adam's fall, until we become born again in water and of the Spirit, our desires and wants will emanate from our bodies and from our souls. Remember that nothing is permanent. Everything can change to the degree that individuals are willing to change.

It is easy to like someone based on his or her outward appearance or behavior, especially in this modern world. People tend to look first at appearances, such as a potential mate's job, wealth, status, and many other worldly things. Then they look at their chemistry, seeking someone suitable and comfortable. I understand it is necessary to look at all aspects of a person's life, but God looks at the heart. God is not particularly interested in the chemistry between two people or either of their appearances. Chemistry and appearances are deceiving and don't last long. When reality strikes, all the superficiality goes away. Only those who stand in truth can stand firm and strong. Listen to what God says in the book of Samuel: "But the Lord said to Samuel, don't judge by his appearance or height, for I have rejected him. The Lord doesn't see things the way you see them. People judge by outward appearance, but the Lord looks at the heart" (1 Samuel 16:7 NLT).

It is understandable that most look at appearances, but be wise enough to see the inside of a person, including the person's honesty, humbleness, and truthfulness. A person can be easily blinded in choosing friends or a partner according to their life conditions. Each one of us is beautifully and wonderfully made, but due to inner sin, many are still under bondage. If anyone turns to God, things start to change in a good way from the inside out. The very nature of the world, until it dies with Jesus, easily stands strong in fulfilling the physical or emotional needs of one's flesh and soul. The human heart may seem right outwardly, but it's the inward spirit of a person that really matters. For out of the heart shall flow springs of life or death, and the nature and character of a person are likewise formed within the heart. Whosoever joins with Christ and obeys His voice will have the nature and character of Christ, and that person will stand on a stable foundation.

When a person becomes born again in Christ for the first time, it takes time for him or her to completely transform into being Christ-like. However, he or she is already on a peaceful road, for one's inner desires and wants quickly start changing into Christ's desires and wants.

I understand that people who don't have Jesus can be humble and obedient in various ways. And people who seem to have Jesus can be stubborn, boastful, and prideful. The issue is not having Jesus or knowing Jesus; it is about whether someone has undergone a complete transformation in Christ and whether that person maintains a life-changing relationship with Him. Satan can be an angel of light, as it says in the Bible. Angels of light seem kind, gentle, and understanding, but that is very deceptive. The focus cannot be self-gain anymore; the focus needs to be your spiritual being going along with Christ the Savior. Humble hearts are what count, for every humble heart is near to God whether it knows Him or not. God gives the most grace to the humble.

Understanding Deeper Where People Stand

Those who don't have a relationship with Jesus may not understand God's way of righteousness and truthfulness. It is hard to lean on that kind of person when it comes to life's reality. Such people will not be able to stand firm with you, guide you, or help you live the way God wants you to live. Good helpers are those who live by the Spirit of God and who hear and know the truth. Also, true love comes from God, and such true love never fails.

Growing up in a Christian home can raise awareness. Someone raised Christian has learned from his or her family. The word of God can activate that person's faith, and that faith can lead the individual to know the truth. Don't just believe what someone tells you. Seek to find the complete truth yourself. There are so many Christians who seem to be good people. They go to church and do what is expected by their pastors or their denominations. They look the part of a Christian, but internally, they are not connected through the Spirit. They find it hard to know the truth, and they spin in circles, constantly wondering how to get out.

I was born in a Christian family that went to church. I looked like I was a good Christian, but inside I didn't even know who Jesus was. I learned the Bible, participated in different programs, and tried to do good things for others. Little did I know that I was far away from God. I didn't know Him until I had a breakthrough in Christ Jesus. My mind was so twisted before that I couldn't understand anything at all, and I have later realized just how stupid and foolish I used to be. When I had the breakthrough, I turned to Him and repented of all my sins. Until I repented, I was a lost sheep living in the darkness and obeying my sinful nature. I know that being born in a Christian family, knowing the Bible, and going to church doesn't mean one is connected to God. Even the devil knows Jesus. Being a good believer is not about knowledge; it is about seeking and worshiping Him in obedience of His commandments. To love God requires a sincere heart.

So, if a person doesn't let God live inside to reign and to rule, how will he or she be able to fulfill his or her given position? Women will not understand how to be good helpers according to God's desire. And if they don't have relationships with Jesus, how can men be righteous and truthful heads of their families? If a man doesn't know how to respect and love the groom, Jesus, then he will not know how to love and respect his wife. This is the same for wives to their husbands, because both are from God. As Paul says, "For as woman came from man, so also man is born of woman. But everything comes from God" (1 Corinthians 11:12 NIV). So, both men and women become helpers to one another in God, for both are the brides of Jesus.

Covenant

It may be easy to mingle with someone who agrees with you, gives you things, and does things with you, but he or she may not necessarily be a good partner for you. When we say "life partner," we mean a lifetime commitment. You can't just throw the partnership away whenever you like. It may be easy to divorce in today's modern world, but pain is pain and hurt is hurt. Pain doesn't change in this modern world. For God, breaking the covenant—the promise—is what really matters. If someone cannot make promises sincerely to his or her earthly spouse, how can he or she be sincere to God? If someone is not serious, I don't think such a person should pursue a relationship for marriage in the first place. Breaking someone's heart may be easy, but healing is slow.

Regrets are painful, hard to forget, and hard to forgive, especially when there is resentment. God doesn't play games. He is serious when it comes to covenants. The choice you make is your choice, not others', and you will pay for or reap from that choice accordingly. Look at how many kids grow up in broken homes and turn to violence. They become aggressive and abusive because of their upbringings. They live in the shadow of their parents' mistakes and sins. Some suffer tremendously, and they may not be able to recover. Children are the future pillars of the kingdom of God. If you build and establish yourself in God, you will build your children—which means you build the kingdom of God. Do not to repeat the same mistake that your parents or grandparents made. Let God help heal the wounds within you before you pursue a relationship. It is good to be wise from the beginning of every friendship, before these friendships become meaningful relationships. If you are already married and are struggling with a wrong partner, seek God's help, for when He touches someone's heart, things turn around. God can cause a complete transformation.

It is important to know and understand God's instructions before you eat of the fruits in the garden. God said, "Choose my instruction rather than silver, and knowledge rather than pure gold. For wisdom is far more valuable than rubies. Nothing you desire can compare with it. I, Wisdom, live together with good judgment. I know where to discover knowledge and discernment. Common sense and success belong to me. Insight and strength are mine" (Proverbs 8:10–12, 14 NIV).

If you are married and want to understand more and want to build your relationship with God, start now. Begin with humbleness unto God. There is nothing too late in God. His love was the same yesterday as it is today and as it will be forever. When you seek Him wholeheartedly, you will find Him, and He will guide and provide for you accordingly. If you have Christ and your partner does not, seek God with fasting and prayer for the one who doesn't have Christ. Don't fight by yourself to make things right; let God handle it. As hard as it gets, hold onto God, stand firm, and walk with faith.

If you already have a broken relationship and have not had any relationship success thus far, stop pursuing man or woman, and instead start pursuing God. The God of peace will provide for you according to your needs in due time. We can never fulfill the desires of another person's heart, and the other cannot fulfill ours either. Only Christ Jesus fulfills. If you are broken in finance or lonely and looking for someone to love, care, provide for, and comfort you, Jesus is the right person. Build yourself first in Him. Be strong and established in Him so that you will be able to help others. As the Bible says, "Seek ye first the kingdom of God, and his righteousness; and all these things shall be added unto you" (Matthew 6:33 KJV).

Seek wisdom and discernment from God, whether you are already invested in a relationship or not. God will guide you in your life journey and will bless you beyond measure (all things shall be added unto you).

In Proverbs, Wisdom says,

I call to you, to all of you! I raise my voice to all people. Listen to me! For I have important things to tell you. Everything I say is right, for I speak the truth and detest every kind of deception. My advice is wholesome.

There is nothing devious or crooked in it. I love all who love me. Those who search will surely find me. I have riches and honor, as well as enduring wealth and justice. My gifts are better than gold, even the purest gold, my wages better than sterling silver! Those who love me inherit wealth. I will fill their treasuries. For whoever finds me finds life and receives favor from the Lord. (Proverbs 8:4–11 NLT)

Sharing and Encouragement: Respect and Honesty

Sharing, encouragement, respect, and honesty work hand in hand. If a person doesn't share how can you encourage him or her, and if the person is not honest, how can he or she be truthful or, by extension, respectful? If the person lacks respect, how can you trust him or her? Such a person will not be able to encourage you in truth or respect you when you share your life story. With respect, a person can open and share honestly once trust has been established.

Sharing, respectful encouragement, and honesty are important for building a strong relationship. If a person is not honest with you before marriage, he or she will not be honest even after marriage. So, how will you know if a person is being honest and genuine with you?

You will be able to know and understand the condition of any person's heart through the time you spend and communicate with him or her. From the person's testimony, actions, lifestyle, and desires, you will be able to discern what is in his or her heart.

Honesty and Respect

What is honesty? Honesty is a facet of morality related to other positive attributes, such as integrity, truthfulness, and straightforwardness. This includes straightforwardness of conduct, the absence of lying, the absence of cheating, the absence of theft, and so on. Honesty also involves being trustworthy, loyal, fair, and sincere. Honesty builds trust and brings the truth to light, which creates freedom for those who hear it. Truth also brings respect.

Being honest in the beginning of knowing someone can be hard for both individuals in a new relationship. You understand that until you are comfortable with the other person, you will not share who you really are; well, the same is true for the other person as well. For some, it may be easy to overcome all things with the love of Christ, but others still struggle to open their lives to others. It is not easy for everyone to reveal his or her life's ups and downs. We are not all comfortable sharing the sin we have committed or the terrible experiences we have had or are currently facing. It will take time, depending on how comfortable both people are with each other.

The book of Romans says, "For all have sinned and fall short of the glory of God" (3:23 NKJV). Each person has a life story to tell. The more I study, the more I spiritually understand that everyone makes mistakes and sins against God one way or the other, and everyone struggles in various ways. Whether everyone commits sin or not, sinful nature works within everyone. It is easy to share the good side of the story, but it's a struggle for many people to share the bad or worse side. Many people will be afraid to share in the first place and will not be comfortable with you until trust has been established.

Be aware of people's differences. Respect and care about people, no matter who they are. Be ready to listen, ready to forgive, and ready to love the way Jesus loves you. Over time, people can get comfortable enough to share more about their personal lives. Communication is the most essential part of building a strong relationship, and communication is not just about exchanging information. It's about respectfully seeking to understand the emotions and intentions behind the information.

From the beginning, my husband and I were open enough to share the deep things in our hearts. We shared from our pasts and from our current lives, opening revealing all our weaknesses and strengths. I love the fact that he makes me comfortable enough to share my heart with honesty and truth. This characteristic brought me great relief and healed me inside and out. He allowed me to build my trust in him, and at the same time, he built his trust in me. Upon that foundation where we started, that foundation of honesty and truth, we still stand together today, which has really helped us solidly bond in our love.

People, for the most part, are sensitive when it comes to sharing their lives. You need to focus on what they share and try to understand their feelings. Don't jump right in, sharing your own thoughts and judging their actions. You might not sin the way they have, but you might be sinning in so many other ways, such as by judging them with pride. Judging others with a prideful heart is the biggest sin in God. Instead, be a good listener. Don't just judge others based on your perspective on what they have said and done. You may not know what they are going through. Communication happens verbally as well as through gestures. So, how can we use gestures to understand one another and help develop our connections?

Gesturing is the body's action! The gesture is a form of nonverbal language or nonverbal communication. The way someone looks at you, listens to you, moves his or her body around you, and reacts to you will tell you more than words alone ever can. Nonverbal communication, or body language, includes facial expressions, bodily movements and gestures, eye contact, posture, tone of voice, and breathing. Developing the ability to understand verbal or nonverbal communication can help you connect with others. Often nonverbal communication expresses what someone really means, which helps you navigate and understand situations involving him or her. Then you can help and encourage him or her to be a better person.

Everyone has a diamond within. That diamond may not shine brightly after difficult life experiences, such as being abused, rejected, oppressed, addicted, angry, bitter, unforgiving, hurt, or enduing many other kinds of hardship, suffering, and struggle. With your help, love, forgiveness, and encouragement, that diamond can shine again. Seek the guidance of the Holy Spirit. Never forget to listen to what the Spirit says in your heart. He will help you know how to encourage and help others in any situation. He will help you build up others positively. Be kind, gentle, and merciful toward them. In truth, that will also help you build yourself up in spirit, which will, in turn, also help build the relationship between the two of you.

3

Relationship Progress: Building Up

Building Trust: Knowing Each Other and Forming a Foundation

How do professional judgments shape a person's personality? For example, if a person is professionally considered broad minded, shy, outgoing, intelligent, or warm, does that outside nature define the person's inner reality? After knowing someone at this outer level, your sense of knowing the person increases until you go to the next level, which is the level of personal concerns and personal life.

Individuals' personal concerns include their personal strivings, life tasks, defensive strategies, and coping skills. At this level, you come to know more details of who the person is, including the person's family, job, interests, roles, plans, goals etc. This develops over time and defines who each person is outwardly. Some quickly are able to know a person, but others take longer. It depends on the time they spend together. But all of this doesn't make you aware of another's identity in life or who they really are.

It is good to know professional judgments of people's personalities, but don't make your judgment based on them, and don't make a quick decision based on outward appearances. The best way is to stand with what you perceive from God. A person's personality can change over time. Knowledge will help you know the differences between outward appearance and inner reality. You also need godly insight to guide and lead you in the right direction. I've seen some of my friends and relatives jump to conclusions just because they like a person based on his or her behavior and nature. They are blinded by the outside beauty and close their minds to the reality of who the person really is inside. Later, they face the consequences, and it is not pleasant.

According to the Bible, "Desire without knowledge is not good—how much more will hasty feet miss the way! A person's own folly leads to their ruin, yet their heart rages against the Lord" (Proverbs 19:2–3 NIV).

Don't move too quickly into fast-paced relationships. Wait until your spirit is ready to accept the relationship's challenges and to take ownership. Don't be like Adam, who loved to live in dominion and power—the headship—without taking the responsibility of asking God's advice or admitted his own fault. Meanwhile, he ate the fruit and blamed Eve. Many act fast, thinking about chemistry based upon outer appearances, but when reality strikes, they break up easily. The regret and shame is damaging and can even destroy one's walk with God. Some later come even to the point of blaming God.

Build Friendship

Focus on building a friendship from the foundation of the Spirit, and the rest will fall into place and eventually satisfy your soul and spirit. People who walk with God can more quickly understand others in Spirit than those who don't walk with God, because the Holy Spirit can reveal all things. If you can see in the Spirit, you will understand a person's uniqueness and quality despite his or her life struggles. You can make the person comfortable enough to trust you because of your genuineness and respect. With that trust, you can build the person up easily as well as will help him or her to reveal his or her heart to you. It is not by your strength that you are going to handle situations but by the power of the Holy Spirit. The Spirit will strengthen you.

Once my mother told me how to look at a situation from a different perspective. She said, "Either you can look at the situation with anger and complain about it or look at the situation with love and bring healing."

So many are reluctant to speak about their personal details to others. However, nothing is too hard when it comes to the right person. It may take some time for things to come out, which is where patience on your part plays a vital role. It is better to share with one another the ups and downs of life before any meaningful relationship begins, because that creates a true foundation upon which a shared life, built on truth, can start. Be willing to forgive and accept one another as Christ accepted you. Your forgiveness and acceptance will wipe away hurt and pain. It will bring healing to one another so that you can start a new life chapter together.

In the beginning, when I came to know the man of my life, I knew from the Spirit that he was the one. Through his word, I understood that he is a man of truth and respect. Furthermore, I saw and can still see in my heart that he is able to help me in my walk with Christ. Likewise, I am able to help him. I also can see his humbleness toward God, which is so peaceful.

Always remember to put God first. Those who pray together and seek God together can make a strong bond in their relationship. No matter how hard it gets at times, choose the right foundation of truth and Spirit; from this foundation streams honesty and trust, which are the backbones that strengthen your relationship.

Intimacy: Waiting on God's Promises

Intimacy includes diverse types of relationship nourishment—emotional, intellectual, physical, and spiritual.

Intimacy needs to exist in a good relationship, but it isn't just about being physical. A good relationship needs emotional, intellectual, and spiritual intimacy; women long for more emotional connections. This kind of nonphysical intimacy will help you feel safe enough to reveal yourselves emotionally in front of each other. Do not start physical intimacy with one another until you have joined the relationship before God in marriage. This can ruin the blessings to come. Be careful. Don't let curses crawl into your relationship by disobeying God and fulfilling lust. In this modern world, we love to do things that are against God's word. How do we believe that nothing will happen to us? That is a lie from the pits of hell! Understand that curses crawl into relationships because of disobedience. Remember that Jesus was the same yesterday, is the same today, and will be the same forever. Don't let your mind be twisted toward any word that is against the word of God.

Emotional, intellectual, and spiritual intimacy are needed whether you are married, in a relationship, or pursuing a relationship. This intimacy allows you to know each other better and to form a stronger bond, which will create a good and strong friendship. Create true friendship, or make your spouse your best friend if you are already married. Best friends share anything and everything from the heart. Best friends help and encourage one another with truth and love, because "a friend loves at all times" (Proverbs 17:17 NKJV).

Emotional and intellectual intimacy are important, but spiritual intimacy is the most important of all because it will build a solid foundation that can last forever. Physical intimacy is only for when you are lawfully married; do not do first what is supposed to be last. Physical intimacy before marriage and outside of marriage is an abomination unto God. The sin of today's world doesn't look like sin anymore to humankind.

As it is written in the Bible, They will say,

""I have the right to do anything," you say—but not everything is beneficial. "I have the right to do anything"—but I will not be mastered by anything. You say, "Food for the stomach and the stomach for food, and God will destroy them both." The body, however, is not meant for sexual immorality but for the Lord, and the Lord for the body." (1 Corinthians 6:12-13 NIV)

If you practice inappropriate physical intimacy, you can repent and seek the Lord's forgiveness before destruction comes. Our God is a good and compassionate God who understands our downfall. He forgives and has accepted those who seek Him wholeheartedly in truth. It is dangerous to do things against the commandment and instructions of the Lord God. We can run away from Satan, but no one can run away from the living God.

Be Disciplined and Obedient in the Lord and Respect One Another

Keep things under control. Do not lead one another to do things at the wrong place and at the wrong time. Regrets in life are not that easy. Every wrong thing has consequences, and everyone pays the price for what he or she has done. One fruit caused many curses through Adam and Eve. It is good to practice self-discipline, self-respect, and obedience in God, even though it's hard. Doing so will bear good fruits in the end, and you will be blessed by your obedience. Do not take things for granted; believe in and receive God's blessings, value it all, and respect others, God, and yourself.

Understand who you are in God, and you will understand the abilities and qualities you received through Him. Then you will not want to just throw it all away like Adam, who sold himself to Satan by not respecting God. Esau also did this to Jacob; a single meal sold his birthright: "You know that afterward, when he wanted his father's blessing, he was rejected. It was too late for repentance, even though he begged with bitter tears" (Hebrews 12:17 NLT). The end of your life may be too late to beg Jesus.

It may be tempting, but with the fear of the Lord, you will obey His desire and will more than your own needs. God created everyone uniquely and wonderfully; we all have our own abilities and qualities. Respect what God gave you with obedience and discipline, and you will know how to respect others. What you do to others can come back to you. Likewise, you will receive the same respect you give others. God gave a commandment for all to obey: "Therefore, all things whatsoever you want men/women should do to you, do ye even so to them: for this is the law and the prophets" (Matthew 7:12 KJV).

In a relationship, respect is more crucial than love and trust. It is required in any stage of a relationship, including yours. Why is respect more important than love? What is respect?

Respect is deep admiration. It requires understanding another's abilities, qualities, and achievements, both great and small. Deep respect comes from having the fear of the Lord. The fear of the Lord makes you respect all His creations, great and small. You not only respect God. You also respect yourself and others. Respect completes the language of love, because when you respect, you obey what is the good and perfect will of God.

When you treat others with respect, that respect can solve many issues and gain the trust of your friend or spouse. Trust is faith; when a person trusts you, that means he or she has faith in you. Faith is the thing you don't see with your eyes but believe can happen. Hold that trust faithfully and respectfully, because once trust is broken, it is hard to get it back.

Trust and respect form a strong bond to one another. In this, it is easy to sacrifice so that good things can happen in each person when a couple is bonded in true love.

True respect comes from the clarity of mind and heart that comes from God. It goes a long way from the time of dating to married life and carries into family life. In any stage of a relationship, if you operate out of respect, the relationship can flow smoothly and enjoy the abundance of what God has given each person. Respect doesn't manipulate others; it promotes the truth and doesn't play games. It doesn't govern with selfish pride or greed; it governs with understanding and humility. Uplifting and strengthening one another fulfills the true meaning of love.

Respecting one another means postponing physical pleasure, especially when you are dating someone. Respect means you will wait for the right time, according to God's desire. If a person doesn't respect you physically, this is a red flag that he or she may not respect you in the future until God transforms the person's heart and mind.

The Bible says, "Be not conformed to this world (worldly fashion and standard): but be ye transformed by the renewing of your mind (by the Holy Spirit), that ye may prove what is that good, and acceptable, and perfect, will of God" (Romans 12:2 KJV).

Commitment and Marriage: Sold Out

Marriage: A Lifetime Commitment

There are many reasons why people get married. What exactly are your thoughts or ideas, and what is the motive or core value informing your desire to get married?

Marriage in God entails two incomplete people helping each other discover God's promises and walking together toward the destiny that God has installed for them since the beginning. God teaches that two are better than one, because they have a good return on their labor. If either of them falls, one can help the other up. And two people can form a *true* relationship from a solid foundation, by helping to build up one another with love and selflessness—just as Christ and His church do.

Marriage is a lifetime commitment, so one should be very careful in choosing a partner. First let us see in the book of Deuteronomy about marriage according to God. The Bible says, "Do not intermarry with them [unbelievers/those who are disobedient to the living God]. Do not give your daughters to their sons or take their daughters for your sons, for they will turn your children away from following me to serve other gods, and the Lord's anger will burn against you and will quickly destroy you" (Deuteronomy 7:3–4 NIV). This is between the children of God and the children of Satan who worship idols. God warned His children by giving a clear commandment not to intermarry with the children of Satan, who are idol worshippers. (Idols can be anything that separates a person from worshiping the living God.)

Remember not to have a limited mind, thinking only about yourself and your own enjoyment, pleasure, or gain. This is about bringing curses into your household that can be there from generation to generation. If there is not early redemption from God the Father, the curses can stay longer. But if you marry someone who is not a believer, and through you, she or he comes to know Christ, what more can we say? So often, instead of you helping the nonbeliever, the nonbeliever pulls you down first. Now you both find yourselves in darkness.

So, the word of God warns everyone by saying,

"Do not be yoked together with unbelievers. For what does righteousness and wickedness have in common? Or what fellowship can light have with darkness? What harmony is there between Christ and Belial? Or what does a believer have in common with an unbeliever? What agreement is there between the temple of God and idols? For we are the temple of the living God. As God has said: I will live with them and walk among them, and I will be their God, and they will be my people. Therefore, Come out from them and be separate, says the Lord. Touch no unclean thing, and I will receive you. I will be a Father to you, and you will be my sons and daughters, says the Lord Almighty." (2 Corinthians 6:14–18 NIV)

We can see that contemporary culture is in a deep crisis regarding marriage and family. As we have seen, the Bible clearly teaches us that God instituted marriage as a covenant between one man and one women. It is the joining of two people in a committed bond for a lifetime—meaning, until death. It is sad that many people cut short their marriages with divorce. The divorce rate in America is forty to fifty percent. Why does this happen? We want the creation, not the creator! Some obey their own choices, fulfilling their own desires, or some marry out of desperation after having been rejected from one relationship to another. Such people run, seeking love, respect, and acceptance from anyone willing to give any out. We may be able to change ourselves to satisfy our needs, but God never changes. His commandments and His words stand firmly—the same yesterday, today, and forever.

Marriage

You might ask what kind of man or woman you would like to marry. Who will be the right person for you? It's kind of hard to even think about it, right? Speculating in our little minds will not help us figure it out.

Marriage is the process by which two people make their relationship public, official, and permanent. That relationship is generally between one man as a husband and one woman as a wife. It is the most intimate human relationship in our lives, and it is a gift from God. It reflects the spiritual relationship between God and humankind. A good relationship is to be pursued and maintained. Do not just sit and expect a good relationship from others or from God. A *solid* relationship is pursued and renewed daily.

The high rate of divorce leaves a mark of fear on the new generations and raises a big question about marriage. It has become a big fear for a lot of people. They think, *Is this the right one, and will it last?* The blessing that is supposed to be free from fear, for the love of God, is now becoming full of fear. To live in fear is not the answer, for God wants everyone to have freedom from fear. Fear is caused by lies. If anyone has a short understanding of truth, that person will be bound with fear. So, what is the truth that can set you free from fear in marriage?

Living and growing up with a lot of pressure from parents, siblings, friends, culture, and society puts a lot of fear in us. The world knows how to bind people with fear. Satan uses those situations to bind people's weaknesses under darkness. Due to the horrible experiences people face in life—experiences that Satan puts them in—many are crushed, broken, and torn inside out. They can't even have the clarity of mind to understand what steps to take, because fear has overtaken them. Some destroy themselves more by choosing the wrong path to healing (such as drugs to numb the pain); instead of fixing it, the problem becomes worse.

The truth is that Satan has tempted people the same way as he tempted Jesus in the Bible. Satan runs hard after people who are still young in faith and innocent. He runs after those who choose the path of Christ by accepting Him as their Savior. He aims to bring them down and then blame them. Jesus understands what everyone goes through and has saved our lives by dying on the cross for us. So, it's not what you have done in the past that matters, and it's not the sin and guilt you carry. It's the new chapter God wants you to have through Jesus; it's His many blessings of peace and freedom.

As the Bible says, "Now the Lord is the Spirit, and where the Spirit of the Lord is, there is freedom" (2 Corinthians 3:17 NIV).

When God says there is freedom in Him, He really means it! Jesus is the healer and the redeemer. If you seek first the kingdom of God and His righteousness, then all other necessary things shall be added unto you. God will add all the things unto you—all His promises. It may look hard to seek God, but it is not hard at all. In fact, you will enjoy Him so much once you come to know Him personally, because He is fun loving, friendly, kind, gentle, and full of love. Once you taste how good God is, you will leave all things to be with Him. Just as you invite your best friend to come over to your house, you can invite Jesus into your life anytime.

My dad was a very loving and kindhearted man, and he taught us a lot of the wisdom he learned from God over the years. He was generous, softhearted, and friendly. But the sin that was instilled in him since the beginning of his life was not blotted out, and it overpowered him. He didn't have the power to overcome the darkness by himself. Even though he earned money for the family, he wasted it on alcohol, gambling, and women. He became violent and abusive toward his wife and his children. Those experiences were really an awakening for me. Every day was a battle for the whole family, and everyone in the family was going through various demonic attacks. Everyone was hurt, and the demon caused a lot of damage internally.

My life was traumatized; I suffered emotionally, mentally, and spiritually. Having experienced those horrible situations, I was torn and devastated, and I suffered tremendously. I was so helpless, and I couldn't understand it fully. People whom I counted on, who seemed to be believers in Christ, abused me mentally and emotionally. They then blamed me for what they struggled with. I was molested and sexually abused, whereas no one seemed to care for me. This caused me to be angry, bitter, and have hatred toward God and Christianity. Several times I wanted to destroy myself, but I didn't. I was blinded until I found Christ. Then the veil was opened for me to see through life to the whys and hows, as God never let go of me.

From the darkness, God helped and transformed me inside and

out. Now I can understand fully that money and power are meaningless without Christ. An empty heart can destroy many lives. These experiences took away my worldly desires in life but transformed my desire in the Lord alone. Also, after years of growing up with those experiences, I made up my mind that instead of marrying a cold-hearted guy, I would rather choose not to marry at all. Not only that, I never believed in myself. I believed I wasn't good enough for others and wondered who would want to marry me. It was crazy, but after welcoming God into my life, things changed. Eight years before my marriage, I heard the voice of the Lord. He spoke to me clearly, saying that He would give me a man whom He was going to bless. I never knew how and when it would happen, and I didn't know who that crazy and blind person could possibly be. Until I met my husband, I was clueless. Within two weeks of knowing him, God showed me in my dreams that he was going to be my husband. I didn't know how it would work; I just had faith in God to help me. Two people coming together from different countries is not a joke. He proposed without knowing what God had showed me, I said yes, and we got married. Even though we face challenges, hardships, and opposition, which can break a relationship, God is with us. Our relationship happens according to the way of God.

God ordained everyone's life before He created the foundation of the world; from the beginning, our destinies and purposes were set according to His glory. When we found Jesus, we found our destinies—our identities—and we found truth, which helps knock out all kinds of fears that come from darkness. Having Jesus in our lives makes our way peaceful and pleasant.

Looking back on my life, every experience I have had, good or bad, reveals to me that everything works together for good. Everything has become a blessing for me. Even my worst experience shaped my life and gave me a double anointing. What Satan took away from me, God means for good and has returned to me with seven times seven blessings. God blessed me with a wonderful man who loves the Lord and who is kind, gentle, peaceful, and merciful. We both live not for our own good but for the kingdom of God, helping those who are brokenhearted and downtrodden. We feed those who are hungry and thirsty for the Lord. We heal all kinds of sickness and set people free from all their bondage by the power of our Lord Jesus Christ. Amen!

Lindsy Rebec Vaiphei Brady

Same-Sex Marriage

It is sad to see our world shaking with people who believe and obey their twisted minds. Due to having different characteristics (man to man and woman to woman), their minds become twisted, and they choose the wrong path. They influence those who are around them, poisoning and being poisoned by worldly nature. They think it's all right to be who they want to be, accepting and embracing same-sex marriage rather than facing the truth. God does not want us to attack those who obey lawlessness but to show them, with love, the truth and the life to set them free. Because they are beautiful and wonderfully created by God, He loves them no matter what. But He wants to transform them according to His promises.

First, everyone knows God doesn't create anyone wrongly. Until people search for Him and His way, their hearts will ponder all the world's questions. This can cause them to make wrong decisions they will regret, and it may be too late for them when they realize it. God made us all flexible enough to be trained in the way He wants us to live. Nothing is too hard to change for a willing heart, soul, and spirit. Developing God's character and nature is earned, though; it is not freely given.

When I was a teenager, I had a friend who was the youngest among three boys. When he was a child, his parents raised him as a girl because they wanted a daughter. His behavior and nature changed slowly: he picked up the feminine side, dressed up like a girl, and talked like a girl. His parents didn't discipline or train him to be the way he should be according to God. He believed that he was a girl and acted just like a girl does. He exchanged his nature for what is against nature: same-sex love. Even though he acts normal outwardly, deep inside he doesn't accept who he is. As he grew up, he didn't have peace and rest; his mind was in a constant battle. He was full of confusion, and he suffered tremendously. Due to the nature of the world he lives in, he was consumed and drawn into the nature, character, and behavior that had taught him. He was deceived and transformed as a transgender person, meaning he obeyed the twisted serpent. But inside he was haunted by his own decision, and he struggled in the absence of peace and joy. Peace and joy come from the fruit of the Holy Spirit, not from the spirit of the world.

God already gave instructions to everyone as it says in the Bible, "Do not be conformed to this world, but be transformed by the renewing of your mind, that you may prove what is that good and acceptable and perfect will of God." (Romans 12:2 NKJV)

But some are stubborn, thinking they can figure out what to do in their lives by themselves. They inevitably choose the wrong path without God. Then they carry sin and guilt in their mixed-up minds. They fall for the wrong people—man for man and woman for woman—which is against God's instruction. So, these people who disobeyed God in biblical times, God abandoned to their foolish thinking, and He gave them up. As it says in the book of Romans,

"For this reason God gave them up to vile passions. For even their women exchanged the natural use for what is against nature. Likewise also the men, leaving the natural use of the woman, burned in their lust for one another, men with men committing what is shameful, and receiving in themselves the penalty of their error which was due. And even as they did not like to retain God in their knowledge, God gave them over to a debased mind, to do those things which are not fitting;" (Romans 1:26-28 NKJV)

Be very careful about this, for it is a fearful thing to fall into the hands of the living God.

Two Become One, Glued Together by Love

Marriage is like two broken pieces joined together with a glue called *love*. The two pieces cannot be healed until they come together. And without the right glue, they cannot stick together. Their own strength is insufficient. The glue is Jesus, who stands between a man and a woman, for God is love. Men and women have their own strong personalities. Without God, those strong personalities can cause a lot of friction and weaken their relationships. But when both submit their weaknesses unto God, the glue of love guides and binds them together with the fullness of joy and satisfaction. This actually depends on how each person carries himself or herself with God. How much does each person submit himself or herself unto the creator and obey Him? This will be reflected in their thinking and conduct toward one another.

Therefore, what God has joined together, let no one separate—including the two of you, husband and wife. You shouldn't tear apart what God has joined together. Every day, there will be a challenge, but with love—with your decision to commit to each other—everything can be conquered.

First, set your mind always on the foundation of truth and honesty in your relationship; that will help you build up your marital life.

Second, love and respect each other no matter what. Don't judge each other's actions, behaviors, and conduct, and don't base the percentage of your love and respect on those actions.

Third, communicate and always apply unconditional love. As hard as it gets, have mercy toward one another, because mercy triumphs over judgment. It is good to be patient and wait upon the Lord in all things, so your joy may be completed in due time.

Married life changes a lot of things; a woman sacrifices to be with her husband, and a husband sacrifices to be with his wife. Both are sold out for one another in the marriage covenant, husband for wife and wife for the husband, just as we are sold out for Christ, our groom. We do not live for our own desires anymore. Where responsibilities and work increase, free time decreases, and life's focus starts changing. The free, single lifestyle, mindset, and choices change; old friends go away; and a time comes for both spouses to cling to each other as best friends. In this, both spouses need more grace, more understanding, more patience, and more humility toward one another to have a happy life together.

When I was newly married, the transition from my old life to my new life was difficult and depressing. Being far away from home and surrounded by all that was unfamiliar was killing me inside; I missed that feeling of familiarity. Stepping out into an unfamiliar place is challenging. During such times, we need a lot of extra love and comfort. I believe this is a place where most women stand when they are newly married. Husbands need to direct extra kindness, patience, and love toward their wives. I believe Eve's life as a newly married woman lead her to the wrong place because Adam wasn't paying much attentions to her. Maybe he continued his old lifestyle after marriage. If they had been glued together inside and outside as husband and wife, I'm sure they would have communicated and made the right decision rather than eat the fruit.

Be kind and patient with one another so that you can stand together (glued with love) as one. This way, there will be no room for the enemy to sneak in.

Intimacy and Satisfaction: Body, Soul, and Spirit

Earlier we discussed emotional, intellectual, physical, and spiritual intimacy. These types of intimacy fall into the larger categories of body, soul, and Spirit intimacy. These are needed in a married life; a husband and wife will face many challenges they have never faced before. They both need to provide grace upon grace to one another.

Look at the three types of intimacy deeper; a couple will need all three in order to fulfill their deepest desires and to satisfy each other. You may be thinking, *Why do they need all three?*

When we think of intimacy, we tend to think of fulfilling the body's desires and satisfying the soul, but we often forget about spiritual intimacy. Spiritual intimacy is the most important of the three, but they are all important. It is good to have balance in life and not to pursue one type of intimacy excessively. Spiritual intimacy means spending individual time with God and then spending time together to fellowship. It means to share spiritual experiences, discuss difficulties inside and outside of life, and spiritually fight the enemy together with prayers. The Bible says, "Do not deprive one another except with consent for a time, that you may give yourselves to fasting and prayer; and come together again so that Satan does not tempt you because of your lack of self-control" (1 Corinthians 7:5 NKJV).

In the beginning of our marriage, our life was hard. I didn't know how we were going to take steps together in God. It was not easy to stand together in prayer and seek the Lord daily. It was a daily battle, and I didn't know how to deal with it. At times it was frustrating and disappointing. I believe most couples face the same thing. Out of frustration, I asked the Lord to show me how we would carry on our life with Him. Then He showed me the life of David from Psalms. David longed to be with the Lord and sought Him day and night. He said,

Early will I seek You; My soul thirsts for You; My flesh longs for You In a dry and thirsty land Where there is no water. So, I have looked for You in the sanctuary, to see Your power and Your glory. Because Your loving-kindness is better than life. My lips shall praise You. Thus, I will bless You while I live; I will lift up my hands in Your name. My soul shall be satisfied as with marrow and fatness, and my mouth shall praise You with joyful lips. When I remember You on my bed, I meditate on You in the night watches. Because You have been my help, therefore in the shadow of Your wings I will rejoice. (Psalm 63:1–7 NKJV)

Isaiah 26:9 speaks of the same longing for the Lord day and night. Since then, I have never stopped seeking the Lord daily. God brought me to a place of living water where I could satisfy my soul and spirit.

My heart was open, so I perceived what the Lord showed me. And early in the morning and late in the evening, my heart longed for Him. It was really hard in the beginning, but nothing comes easy in this world. With time, things changed. Our daily life is now full of excitement and joy. Being with the Lord makes it easy to battle every obstacle or hardship the enemy places in our lives. My husband and I, we love to spend time with the Lord, and we love to share the revelations and miracles that He gives us. The peace and joy we have cannot be compared with anything on earth. We live without tension between us, and our home is like heaven on earth, full of peace. God gives us the strength we need in life. His revelations give us understanding, which brings joy and satisfaction. It is amazing to be in the presence of God; we may be weak, but He is strong!

Bodily intimacy lasts for few minutes, and the soul's intimacy lasts longer, but spiritual intimacy lasts forever. When a couple stands together in the same Spirit, they do not look at each other lustfully; instead, they look at each other with the deepest love. And that changes their minds, bodies, and souls. When their spirits are joined together, their bodies and souls also connect. Then they both can enjoy intimacy to the fullest in body, soul, and spirit.

With an understanding of the depth of the Spirit, your intimacy will be more satisfying, joyful, and fulfilling. Rather than fulfill one another's needs (as needs become a law), it will become a beautiful close-knit love relationship. Indeed, the Spirit overcomes the law.

Sold Out to One Another

Be sold out to one another for the benefit of your marriage. There should not be room for pride and selfishness. There are immature believers in Christ who set rules and regulations—what to do and what not to do. Such rules are not led by the Spirit but led by the law. Paul wants them to understand that marital life is to practice *selflessness* in the body, soul, and spirit, which means to be sold out to one another. Selflessness comes into place when we practice humility, and humility is a great sacrifice.

An example of when we sold out was when we accepted Christ as our Savior. We became His, for He redeemed us—bought us for a price—from sin and death. We need to be completely obedient to Him. If anyone doesn't sell out to Christ, he or she cannot have complete transformation or complete life in Him. This means the person is still holding the past (old leaven bread), which hinders the person's present and future lives. God wants everyone to be sold out to Him, He wants us to be new unleavened bread, completely born again, so that He will be able to bless everyone abundantly without any hindrance. Likewise, a husband and wife both need to be sold out to each other for the glory of God. If they are holding their pasts in in their marital life, they cannot go forward into a successful, happy marriage.

After the wedding and celebration, you both will be excited to discover more of each other. Enjoy this blissful moment of living, traveling, sightseeing, and engaging in every form of enjoyment you can think of. It is a peak time of life, full of fun, excitement, adventure, and energy—until you have another adventure, which is having kids. In every stage of life, if you both continue holding onto God, you will discover more adventures through which you can enjoy every bit of life together with God.

God created each of us to be flexible enough to learn, move, and act. We not only have physically flexibility or mental flexibility but also spiritual flexibility. God wants us to learn and acquire wisdom and understanding from Him. He wants us to keep on growing, not to stop because everyone is still alive. He doesn't want us to be limited or to stop growing, as He is not a limited God. If anyone is open enough to try and learn, anything is possible. Even the impossible, with Him, is possible.

Paul says, "The wife does not have authority over her own body but yields it to her husband. In the same way, the husband does not have authority over his own body but yields it to his wife" (1 Corinthian 7:4 NIV). When Paul said *body*, this can be read as everything within the body, including flesh, soul, and spirit. Paul addresses that it is good to share thoughts, ideas, love, and every aspect of life, for life is not a solitary experience anymore. He told them not to selfishly conduct their own lives but to share and to give way to one another because it is better to give than to receive.

Satan tempted Eve and Adam because of their lack of communication and sharing; they seemed to furthermore have no communication with the Father in heaven. The weakness or strength of a husband is the weakness or strength of his wife; the same is true in reverse for the wife. Everything reflects that no one can separate from a marriage, as the two are already one. How beautiful it is if both understand and stand together for the goodness of one another! Their sacrifice means that the joy of the Lord will rest upon them. As the Bible says, "There is no greater love than to lay down one's life for one's friends" (John 15:13 NLT) So, "be completely humble and gentle; be patient, bearing with one another in love. Make every effort to keep the unity of the Spirit through the bond of peace" (Ephesians 4:2–3 NIV).

Be Strong, for the Enemy Is Roaming around to Devour You

You and your partner may not always see fireworks like you did in the early stages of your relationship. The key is not to freak out. There are many couples that are just roommates because they live together in a room but are separated in their hearts. Some sleep in one bed but are separated in soul and spirit. Everyone knows relationships are hard and take effort to maintain, and sometimes they disappoint. Paul understands that people struggle, and he understands that a husband and wife will not be able to survive together with their own strength. He knows they both need strength from God to renew their thoughts and refresh their minds.

God highlights how important it is to spend intimate time with Him so that He will be able to help both understand each other. He can provide insights that will help each to love the other unconditionally and to stand together in hardship and in struggle. It is good for the husband to love God more than his wife, just as it is good for the wife to love God more than her husband. God can then glue the two of you together as one in Christ.

Paul knows that physical and soul desires will soon pass away and face reality. You see, many couples break up after several months or years, and the brokenhearted go from one relationship to another to satisfy their needs. They will continue to break one marriage to the next until they learn that love is not just about them and their needs. Love is not about fulfilling their own selfish desires; it is about obedience to help others in God. Due to the many broken marriages and broken relationships, there are many rebellious children today. They rebel because of a lack of love.

When parents are so busy satisfying their needs, how can they satisfy the needs of their children? Love is not money or what you can provide (provision is a bonus). Love is *discipline, commitment,* and *sacrifice.* Life is short. No one knows how long he or she will live here on earth. Some are so busily absorbed in their own lives that they don't realize how much time goes by. They miss out on God's promises of blessing before their time here comes to an end.

For couples to stay strong, they both need to be in line and to first seek the kingdom of God. Physical and soul needs are extras in a married life; God wants you to have good things, according to His way. But if you are not seeking God fervently and are running after fulfilling your own desire, Satan is ready to take away all your blessings. You are supposed to get your blessings from God. If you open the door for the enemy to lead you to excess, he will destroy you and your family. Give time to God so that you will have wisdom and understanding. That will shut the door of Satan in your life and for generations to come.

Unconditional Love and Respect: Cherish and Recognize One Another

Jesus is the life-giving Spirit, and whoever has Jesus within has that Spirit of life within as well. Living into the light of Jesus is freedom from all kinds of darkness. Darkness binds the body, soul, and spirit. Spouses need to believe that victorious, beautiful Christian marriages are in the grasp of all who invite Jesus to be the centerpiece of their love stories. Make

Jesus Christ your first love; as discussed earlier, He is the perfect glue to bind two together with peace. Life is not always predictable, marriage isn't always perfect, and there is no perfect husband or perfect wife, but you can make anything perfect through Christ's love.

As the Bible says, "Speaking the truth in love, you will grow to become in every respect the mature body of Him who is the head, that is, Christ. From Him the whole body, joined and held together by every supporting ligament, grows and builds itself up in love, as each part does its work" (Ephesians 4:15–16 NIV).

The Bible also says, "Love is patient and kind, not jealous or boastful or proud or rude. It does not demand its own way. It is not irritable, and it keeps no record of being wronged. It does not rejoice about injustice but rejoices whenever the truth wins out. Love never gives up, never loses faith, is always hopeful, and endures through every circumstance" (1 Corinthians 13:4–7 NLT). Many find this hard to apply in their lives, but it's not that hard when they know the truth and when that truth is rooted in them. It is not physical exercise that brings out the love, according to the word; it is the Spirit flowing in you that will shine out. It's not about forcing yourself to love your spouse because of what the Bible says. It's about knowing and understanding the decision you made—"the seal of the promised." Stand firm in your promises, respecting your decision and sacrificing for the love of Christ Jesus, who is the author and the finisher of your faith.

Love never manipulates, criticizes, insulates, or abuses. It is patient, full of grace, and merciful. True love (agape love, which is Christ Jesus) will change your heart, which will change your perspective. Love is special, beautiful, and wonderful. It is emotional as well as intellectual, physical, and spiritual. It can penetrate deep inside bone and marrow. You can feel it inside your spirit, soul, and body. No one can have or achieve that love without the Holy Spirit of God. It is not by your strength or by your power but by the Holy Spirit that you experience true love, says the Lord.

God's ways are indeed a mystery, and it is impossible for everyone to know and understand fully the deep things of God without His Holy Spirit; the Holy Spirit reveals things, even the deepest things of God. You will know and understand them when you hear and listen to Him.

Appreciation

The greatest joy for a person, young or old, is when others recognize his or her achievements. It is a joyful reward for that person, and it increases his or her ability and confidence. As is advised by the Bible, "Do not withhold good from those to whom it is due, when it is in the power of your hand to do so (Proverbs 3:27 NKJV).

Appreciate one another, even in small things. That will help uplift one another. Don't take one another for granted. Don't treat each other as commoners. Know that each of you is created wonderfully by God and that He loves and respects your spouse the same way He loves and respect you. When Boaz allowed Ruth to gather grain in his fields, she thanked him for his kindness. In return, Boaz honored Ruth for all she had done to help her mother-in-law, Naomi, saying, "May the Lord, the God of Israel, under whose wings you have come to take refuge, reward you fully for what you have done" (Ruth 2:12 NLT). No matter who someone is, where the person comes from, or whether the person is poor or rich, if you show kindness to him or her, you show kindness to God. In return, God will bless you abundantly.

As a couple, it is important to recognize one another's achievements, whether small or great. Whether you are a stay-at-home mom or a working wife, if your husband recognizes your efforts and sacrifices, what a joy it will be. The same goes for a wife who recognizes her husband's challenging work, his love, his dedication, and all the things he is doing. How good is it for him to hear that?

You should uplift each other, whatever your stage of life. You shouldn't do it because this book says so; do it because you see it in your heart. Show your unconditional love and appreciation with deep understanding from the Spirit. If you love your spouse, you love yourself. Love should not be as simple as words coming out of your mouth and into the wind. It's not only the words you speak from your mind; it should come from within the heart with an action.

In today's world, people water down the word *love*. It has lost its power as a word. Love is not selfish. Love is patient, comforting, peaceful, and healing when used correctly. Love should not be applied only when you need something from your spouse. Love is sincere, understanding, caring, selfless, sacrificial, and unconditional. It is not selfish. It is selfless. Love is doing things without expectation of anything in return. It is doing to others what you want them to do to you, and it is doing so with Christ-like selflessness.

Comforting Each Other

When God puts something together, it only gets better with time. When Jesus builds a lifelong romance between husband and wife, He saves the best for both. The most comforting thing for a wife is when the husband shows his true loving word from his heart. I love when my husband lovingly hugs me and speaks to me from his heart. His loving words comfort and heal me. It is comforting when a husband and wife stand together in Christ no matter what.

I love to be with my husband. He is my best friend, and I can share anything with him. He listens to me attentively when I share my inner heart, and he encourages and guides me in the right way. What a joy it is to have someone whom you trust. Listening to others with love is healing. I was healed inside and out through him. I too learned how to listen to others through him, and now I do the same for him and others. People love to talk, but I see few who like to listen. The word of God says, "Let everyone be swift to listen, slow to speak and slow to become angry" (James 1:19 NIV). Listening to others attentively is one way of showing how you love them. It is also teaching oneself self-discipline and self-sacrifice in the Lord.

What God wants from a husband is to love his wife as his own body, because God knows how much a woman longs for love from her husband. Love is not something you can just understand, because it doesn't come from the flesh. It comes from the Spirit of God. Love is one of the fruits of the Holy Spirit, and those who don't have the Spirit of God cannot understand true love. It is the Spirit of God who reveals the heart of true love. Let people understand the real meaning of true love, because true loves builds up rather than tears down. Living in the Holy Spirit, you will learn in due time how to be humble, patient, and kind, and you will know how to love others as God loves you. With the Holy Spirit, it is easy to respect one another in a relationship, which will help you build a stronger relationship. Make your spouse your best friend. Don't let anything stand between the two of you except for Jesus, who is the real love.

Respect and love are not selfish. When God says to respect, He means without condition, much as He tells children to respect (obey) their parents. God wants us to do things unconditionally, without any selfish expectations. A respectful wife expects to get love from her husband, and a loving husband expects to get respect from his wife. Without conditions, love and respect one another, for you are a son and daughter of God.

The Bible advises, "Husbands, love your wives just as Christ loved the church and gave his life for it [unconditional love]. Men ought to love their wives just as they love their own bodies. A man who loves his wife loves himself, also it applies to both that women must love and respect her husband, same as husband must love and respect his wife: every husband must love his wife as himself, and every wife must respect her husband" (Ephesians 5:25, 28, 33 GNB).

Submission

The Bible says, "Be of the same mind toward one another. Do not set your mind on high things, but associate with the humble. Do not be wise in your own opinion" (Romans 12:16 NKJV).

Submission or subjection can be hard for anyone, especially those who live with lawlessness (disobedience to God's instructions). A lot of people, as we know, are too proud and overconfident. They think so highly of themselves that they think they can do things whenever and however they want. Humanity is the most stubborn and hardheaded creation among all creations because of our ability to be like God, but few understand that they are the weakest among all creation without God. Men and women should not be measured unequally, for God sees and judges them the same.

Let's look at women. Some are independent and can do things without their husbands. They can earn more money or become richer than their husbands. They think they can become better than their husbands and try to put their husbands under their control. Meanwhile, other women are victims to their husbands' controlling spirits and are taken for granted because they are the weaker vessels. And some husbands who should be in control of themselves work so hard to please their wives or families that they put their trust in themselves instead of trusting God. Life can become so chaotic that sometimes it's hard to have a clear mind or remember how to solve problems.

God already knows the ways of humankind. That is why He gave us a *standard of operations* by which we can live orderly lives and be blessed. The first standard of operations is to submit to Him fully so that He can lead and guide us out of problems and troubles in this sinful world. This standard of operations is His commandment, and His instruction is from the living word. He provided His Spirit (the helper) to reveal all things inside our hearts. These instructions or commandments are not an option; they are the truth we need to follow and obey for our own good. It is good for everyone to find out this truth and understand why He said it so that everyone can receive all the hidden treasures. But this hidden treasure cannot be received easily without sincere and obedient submission to Him.

When God says *submit*—which holds whether rich or poor, famous or not, good or bad, strong or weak—all must submit under His authority with a sincere heart. As it said in the word, every knee shall bow down to Him without exception. So, no one can fully understand submission until he or she comes under the subjection and authority of Jesus. Submission is obedience toward an authority. When God says *submit* or *subject*, He means to humble oneself—to make oneself weak. When God says, "Submit unto Me," He knows that without humbleness it's hard to submit to God. When a wife humbles herself, it means that she shouldn't do as she likes. She should have a mutual understanding with her husband that comes from the guidance of the Lord. Husbands, the bride of Jesus, must humble themselves to Jesus. As, "The husband is the head of the wife, as Christ is the head of the church, and He is the Savior of the body" (Ephesians 5:23 NKJV). All must work together with the fear of the Lord and with sincere hearts. God is orderly, and His instructions help us live orderly lives full of freedom and peace.

Humility is a great sacrifice, as humility crucified the desires and wants of the body and soul. Husband and wife are equal in the eyes of God. God wants both to work together for His glory. Even though both are equal, He gives different responsibilities and tasks to each in order to fulfill His plan. This may be hard at times to accept, especially when two ideas, wants, desires, or choices are involved. However, it is not that hard in any situation if both are patient toward one another and run after God's heart. They can make decisions based on what is right and true.

God gave women special responsibilities, and in this, He also gave women an extraordinary gift—*insight*. Insight means to see things deeper than what others see. Men operate on various levels of governing, authority, power, and dominion, but they are lacking in insight. Women can use their insight to bring back men's lost connections to God. The Bible says women should use their insight from God by manifesting gentle hearts and quiet spirits rather than worrying about their outside appearance. Men find it harder to humble themselves toward God than women do. Thankfully, women have power over men to help them humble themselves before God because of their God-given insight. The gift of the Holy Spirit is feminine, which is why men find it harder to understand. Women were born with that quality. The Bible says, "House and wealth are the inheritance from fathers, but a wise, understanding, and sensible wife is [a gift and blessing] from the Lord" (Proverbs 19:14 AMP). Men build a house, but women build a home.

Commandments for Husbands, Wives, and Children, According to God: Decision-Making

Without following the instructed road, no one can achieve the promises of God. No matter how much you try to fix your relationship to make it unbreakable, you will not achieve it without Christ, the solid Rock, who laid out the way for everyone with instructions to obey.

God the Father in heaven is so loving that He understands and has put all things together before the foundation of the world. He understands the difficulties people come across. He gave specific instructions for everyone so that all will be able to enjoy beautiful lives together. His instructions are not too hard for everyone to obey.

God said,

"This commandment I am giving you today is not too difficult for you, and it is not beyond your reach. It is not kept in heaven, so distant that you must ask, "Who will go up to heaven and bring it down so we can hear it and obey?" It is not kept beyond the sea, so far away that you must ask, "Who will cross the sea to bring it to us so we can hear it and obey?" No, the message is very close at hand; it is on your lips and in your heart so that you can obey it." (Deuteronomy 30:11–14 NLT)

When you know the truth about men, women, and children according to God's perspective, you can easily understand each other better as a family or as a whole. He teaches us about raising our kids the way He wants them to be (not our way but His way). He has given us the foundation. Just as each spouse has responsibilities at home, the children also have their own responsibilities in a family.

The Commandment for Men

As a husband and a father in the house: "Husbands, love your wives, just as Christ also loved the church and gave Himself for her, that He might sanctify and cleanse her with the washing of water by the word, that He might present her to Himself a glorious church, not having spot or wrinkle or any such thing, but that she should be holy and without blemish. So husbands ought to love their own wives as their own bodies; he who loves his wife loves himself. For no one ever hated his own flesh, but nourishes and cherishes it, just as the Lord does the church. For we are members of His body, of His flesh and of His bones." (Ephesians 5:25-30 NKJV)

"Husbands, in the same way be considerate as you live with your wives, and treat them with respect as the weaker partner and as heirs with you of the gracious gift of life, so that nothing will hinder your prayers." (1 Peter 3:7 NIV) Do not be embittered or resentful toward them, because of the responsibilities of marriage. "So be happy with your wife and find your joy with the woman you married — pretty and graceful as a deer. Let her charms keep you happy; let her surround you with her love." (Proverbs 5:18-19 GNB)

Respect and love your wife, encourage her, and enjoy her as a blessing from God. Let your respect not be defined by her character and nature. Have a noble and graceful character, walking with wisdom and understanding. Be faithful and righteous so that you will bless your children through the example you show.

"And, ye Parents, provoke not your children to wrath: but bring them up in the nurture and admonition of the Lord." (Ephesians 6:4 KJV) The book of Colossians says, "Fathers/Mothers, do not provoke or irritate or exasperate your children [with demands that are trivial or unreasonable or humiliating or abusive; nor by favouritism or indifference; treat them tenderly with lovingkindness], so they will not lose heart and become discouraged or unmotivated [with their spirits broken]." (Colossians 3:21 AMP) .

The Commandment for Women

As a wife and a mother in the house, "Wives, submit yourselves unto your own husbands, as unto the Lord. For the husband is the head of the wife, even as Christ is the head of the church: and he is the saviour of the body. Therefore as the church is subject unto Christ, so let the wives be to their own husbands in everything." (Ephesians 5:22-24 KJV)

"In the same way, you wives must accept the authority of your husbands. Then, even if some refuse to obey the Good News, your godly lives will speak to them without any words. They will be won over by observing your pure and reverent lives. Don't be concerned about the outward beauty of fancy hairstyles, expensive jewellery, or beautiful clothes. You should clothe yourselves instead with the beauty that comes from within, the unfading beauty of a gentle and quiet spirit, which is so precious to God. This is how the holy women of old made themselves beautiful. They put their trust in God and accepted the authority of their husbands." (1 Peter 3:1-5 NLT)

"Wives, be subject to your husbands [out of respect for their position as protector, and their accountability to God], as is proper and fitting in the Lord. (Colossians 3:18 AMP)

To submit is to subordinate—not as inferior but out of respect for the responsibilities entrusted to husbands and their accountability to God. Partner with them. Some husbands who do not obey the word of God may be won over to Christ because of their wives' godly lives. Their modest and respectful behavior with their devotion and appreciation in God may bring their husbands to Christ. Respect and love your husband, encourage him, and enjoy him as a blessing from God. Let your respect not be defined by his character and nature. Have a noble and graceful character, walking with wisdom and understanding. Be faithful and righteous so that you will bless your children through the example you show.

"And, ye Parents, provoke not your children to wrath: but bring them up in the nurture and admonition of the Lord." (Ephesians 6:4 KJV) The book of Colossians says, "Mothers/Fathers, do not provoke or irritate or exasperate your children [with demands that are trivial or unreasonable or humiliating or abusive; nor by favoritism or indifference; treat them tenderly with lovingkindness], so they will not lose heart and become discouraged or unmotivated [with their spirits broken]." (Colossians 3:21 AMP)

The Commandment for Children

"Children, obey your parents in the Lord [that is, accept their guidance and discipline as His representatives], for this is right [for obedience teaches wisdom and self-discipline]. H ONOR [esteem, value as precious] YOUR FATHER AND YOUR MOTHER [and be respectful to them]--this is the first commandment with a promise-- SO THAT IT MAY BE WELL WITH YOU, AND THAT YOU MAY HAVE A LONG LIFE ON THE EARTH." (Ephesians 6:1-3 AMP)

"'Honor (respect, obey, care for) your father and your mother, as the LORD your God has commanded you, so that your days [on the earth] may be prolonged and so that it may go well with you in the land which the LORD your God gives you." (Deuteronomy 5:16 AMP)

Let your obedience should not be defined by your parents' characters and natures. *Honor* your parents, esteem them, and value them as precious gifts from God.

Children, obey your parents in all things, for this is well pleasing to the Lord." (Colossians 3:20 NKJV)

> ➤ Satan knows the word of God. He uses it against God by destroying many children's lives. When children's upbringing is abusive and broken, they will carry this for a long time. And by the time they realize the truth to set them free, they may have hurt many others the way they were hurt. Comfort and peace for a child is not money or material gifts supplied by their parents. Comfort is to see

their parents standing together as one and lovingly sacrificing their lives for their children. As everyone knows, "Foolishness is bound in the heart of a child; the rod of correction [love] shall drive it [that foolishness] far from him" (Proverbs 22:15 KJV). That rod of correction will bring wisdom in their lives, which will be a shield of protection, and they will not depart from it when they are old.

➤ Disobeying the commandment of God because of a selfish heart brings disorder. When someone is not concerned with the things of the Lord but is consumed by life and the world, the love of God is not in him or her, and his or her life will go downhill. The worst thing is that the person alone will not face the problem; the person brings it wherever he or she goes, whether inside or outside the family. God desires all to work together in unity, peace, and harmony. He wants all to have blessed lives by operating within the orderly love of God. Make the environment more lovely and peaceful by knowing and understanding the way of the Lord. Behave with an orderly conduct according to God's way.

For all, in all things, do the following:

First, obey the first and the greatest commandment of God, "Love the Lord your God with all your heart and with all your soul and with all your mind." (Matthew 22:37 NIV) Learn the fear of the Lord by worshiping Him with all your heart, with all your soul and with all your mind. Then, once you obey this, the rest of all other commandments will fall in place for God gave humankind step-by-step instructions to train ourselves well for our blessing. Know that He is the FIRST and the LAST.

Family, As in Christ

In the Bible, the husband is called the head of the family, and women are the helpers (the backbones). When the head gets a headache, the rest of the body can still walk, work, and run. But when the backbone hurts, the whole body cannot function properly. Heal the back (the helper). The head is also called the "leader," which comes with high responsibility. Let's look at Genesis to read what responsibility God gave Abraham (the head): "For I [God] have chosen him, so that he will direct his children and his household after him to keep the way of the Lord by doing what is right and just, so that the Lord will bring about for Abraham what he has promised him" (Genesis 18:19 NIV). This is an instruction from God to humankind (legacy).

Generally, men are stronger outside than inside until they have God inside them. Without Christ, their insides can be weak, but due to their strong and powerful characters, this doesn't show outwardly. Also, they don't want to admit that they are weak and broken. It's harder for them to show they are in pain. They are also weak in communication, so forming a good relationship with God or family is hard for them to do. For women, communication is their strength, and it's easy for them to form a bond between families. They are like a bridge or a backbone between everyone.

We already know women are more sensible, compassionate, gentle, and emotional than men, but that doesn't mean that men don't have those characteristics inside. It is a little hard for men to express themselves as well as women can. However, they both fight the battle in dealing with those different emotions they carry because of their characters and natures. God is teaching men to be gentle with women and to respect them for who they are, because men can easily destroy women by using their manly sides. They can easily abuse women's weaknesses by using their masculinity. Women likewise should not use their weaknesses to pull down men's strength like Eve. Men are mostly boastful and prideful because of their dominion and governing nature instincts. They love showing their masculine side and are not necessary aware of the feminine side of God. Women can use their feminine side to get what they want and to bring men under their authority, which contradicts God's will for women as well.

This is the will of God. When God put woman in man's life, He knew already that through woman, man can start learning and experiencing the softer side of God. Also, God wants man to have complete transformation inside and out through the example set by woman. In a woman's good conduct and gentle spirit, with her purity and reverence of life, women must not use outward appearances for power over men. God knows the quality of women and what women can do to men whom God loves. Is God against jewelry or hairstyles? No. Peter speaks clearly to every woman and wife to be submissive to the husband so that they will be able to help husbands inwardly. Husbands will be able to understand submission through women because most men are not strong in understanding inwardly how to submit to God. If women use outward appearances for power, they will get attention that is sensual and demonic, but if they use their inner selves, they will get attention inwardly, which is spiritual. Men can easily obey their women more than God, just as Adam obeyed Eve. The book of Peter understands that women hold the right tools to bring men back to God, and through them, husbands will have restored all that they had lost in the hands of Satan. Then, they both will be able to stand together in Christ, and they both will set an example for their children (helping the next generation to find God).

So, how important is the backbone in helping the body stay strong together? The mother/wife is the strength of the household who supplies strength to the husband/father and the children. As the Bibles says, "A wise woman builds her home, but a foolish woman tears it down with her own hands" (Proverbs 14:1 NLT). Everyone can build a house but not home; a home needs wisdom to build it. A wise women submits with respect to her husband, for the husband stands in the higher authority, which represents God. Likewise, the husband loves his wife like Christ loves the church, for women are the weaker vessels. Women and the Holy Spirit (both helpers) are very sensitive, so don't grieve or make them sad.

As it says in the book of Peter, "Husbands, in the same way be considerate as you live with your wives, and treat them with respect [honor them] as the weaker partner and as heirs with you of the gracious gift of life, so that nothing will hinder your prayers" (1 Peter 3:7 NIV).

Women seem to have more insight (spiritual wisdom) than men because of their inner spirits given by God. The word of God says, "Blessed are those who find wisdom, those who gain understanding, she is more precious than rubies; nothing you desire can compare with her. Long life is in her right hand; in her left hand are riches and honour. Her ways are pleasant ways, and all her paths are peace. She is a tree of life to those who take hold of her; those who hold her fast will be blessed." (Proverbs 3:13, 15-18 NIV)

Also, it says, "He who finds a wife finds what is good and receives favor from the Lord" (Proverbs 18:22 NIV) Because of the helpful nature a woman has. The woman strengthens the husband, and the Holy Spirit strengthens both the husband and wife, inside and out with wisdom and understanding.

Paul asks everyone to put hope in positive and spiritual things:

"Is there any encouragement from belonging to Christ? Any comfort from His love? Any fellowship together in the Spirit? Are your hearts tender and compassionate? Then make me truly happy by agreeing wholeheartedly with each other, loving one another, and working together with "one mind and purpose" (in Christ). Don't be selfish; don't try to impress others. Be humble, thinking of others as better than yourselves. Don't look out only for your own interests, but take an interest in others, too. You must have the same attitude that Christ Jesus had: "Though he was God, he did not think of equality with God as something to cling to. Instead, he gave up his divine privileges; he took the humble position of a slave and was born as a human being. When he appeared in human form, he humbled himself in obedience to God and died a criminal's death on a cross" (Philippians 2:1–8 NLT).

Be completely humble. Be patient toward one another and ready to forgive each other no matter what. Be merciful, courteous, kind, gentle, and tenderhearted to one another. Remember the grace of God that was given to you. Let that grace of God be upon others as well. I understand when things do not go according to our expectations, the fire inside of our heart burns easily. We act fast to make things the way we want, but God is in charge. Obey the commandments given by God in Spirit and in truth so that you will have abundant life on earth and in heaven.

It is good to submit to God and to submit to one another without any hidden secret (no yeast). Be open and share everything and help each other to heal and restore. The more the husband loves his wife, the more the wife respects him. The more she respects her husband, the more he loves her. Standing together as one, they both can train their children in the right way. Parents are the greatest examples to their children, for parents stand in place of God on earth. Children can see God through them.

Daily Decision-Making

Decision-making as a family can be quite challenging because of the different responsibilities, characters, and individual natures. Before any decision is made, it is good to know the different natures in the family, because a person can make any decision emotionally, without God's will. It is good to examine all things in truth, as by doing so, you will have peace in what the right decision is.

Everyone makes decisions daily; some decisions are made quickly without much thought, and some take longer. Quick decisions are like the clothes you are going to wear, the breakfast or the dinner you are going to eat (even though at times that is hard), and the trivial things that emerge from daily routines. Some decisions are forced upon you in the most difficult and stressful times and are harder than the usual decisions.

Most decisions have a short or lasting impact in your life. The best thing to do as a couple is to discuss and talk about it and then see what the best way is. Someone may have to compromise. If it is really a hard situation, pray to God and seek His direction. Discussion can also bring trouble if both do not understand the other's motives or take differences personally. To have a peaceful agreement that works is very challenging at times, especially when each person's wants are different. Always hear what the Spirit says in your heart, and act according to what God wants for both of you.

Try to discover the truth together—such as what the outcome will be—and don't try to push your own interests. That will help your marriage mature and stay strong and happy. It is important to remind yourself where you stand (your foundation). It may not be necessary for your decisions to always be right. Be flexible enough to stretch your understanding of the other person's point of view. Sometimes the issues are big for you, but when seeing further and deeper, something may not be that important anymore. When we moved to a new house, we needed some furniture. My idea of buying furniture was so different from my husband's. What I liked he didn't like, and what he liked I didn't like. It was kind of a battle until I asked the Lord. The Lord told me that He had a better choice. Within a few months, during which I patiently waited, God brought us to the right place. God's favor was upon us, and the store we went to gave us a special discount that they typically never give. We both are quite satisfied with what we got. Now every time we see that furniture, we remember God's favor and what a blessing it is.

It is good to make one another comfortable enough to share and discuss issues. Encourage each other, and freely share your thoughts, feelings, and opinions with love, respect, and kindness. Avoid criticism, control, or dominion over each other. Try your best not to be offended or take things personally; it will create more strife and stress. Be careful to monitor your attitude and tone of voice. If underneath your words is criticism, disrespect, or sarcasm, your spouse will hear it easily, so let kindness, gentleness, and love flow through you.

Some love to talk more, but it is good to listen attentively. After all, we have two ears to hear and one mouth to talk. When your spouse talks, listen without interruption, and request clarification if needed with a gentle heart and spirit. Always strive for unified and peaceful decisions, even if it takes a longer time. Attentively listening to one another brings you together in harmony and understanding.

As the Bible instructs, "Trust in the Lord with all your heart and lean not on your own understanding; in all your ways acknowledge and submit to him, and he will make your paths straight" (Proverbs 3:5–6 NIV).

5

Challenges and Difficulties: Tests

Temptations, Hardships, and Challenges: Misunderstandings

Married life has a lot of challenges, difficulties, and problems because it is two in one—two minds and two hearts come together as one. If root causes of problems are not solved or not blotted out, this can cause major issues for a couple. It can become so bitter that it causes separation or divorce. In between spouses, the most common argument is a result of misunderstanding and poor communication. Many times, it's nobody fault. Rather, it's a simple misunderstanding of one another's point of view.

It's easy to believe that your relationship is different from everyone else's. It's probably not. Relationships take effort to maintain, and you won't always be happy with your partner, even though you both love each other. When a relationship is brand new, loving your spouse may come easy. You're still curious and discovering more about each other. It seems easy to grow together as a couple at first. But eventually, reality hits you, and you're bound to encounter some roadblocks that will test your faith, love, and connection with your spouse.

Inside and outside of a Christian's life, whether in married or personal life, challenges and difficulties are everywhere. But it seems that more challenges come in a Christian family or a believer's life than in unbelievers' lives. Let's look at this happening among believers. Christians' divorce rate might be higher than any other religion's, and there are more broken families in Christian society then any other society! A lot of people wonder why. When you look at your life as a believer in Christ, you often wonder, where is God? You ask this because of the challenges, the hardships, and the suffering you've seen. Many leave their faith and walk away from God because of the hardships they have had to endure. Not having an understanding of the self causes this.

Look at this story: A spouse says to the other spouse, "I love you, but I'm not in love with you, and I can't live with you anymore" or "I love another person." Sometimes it doesn't make sense. Love has character; without that character, it's empty. It's like a child saying to the parents, "I love you," without knowing the real meaning; it is like being gone with the wind.

Root Causes of Problems

Some of the root causes of problems inside and outside of a relationship follow:

- Personal differences
- Home chores
- Lack of communications
- Stress
- Unrealistic expectations
- Comparisons to the other spouse
- Money/finance manipulations
- Lack of intimacy
- Inappropriate priorities
- Lack of concern
- Infidelity
- Miscarriage
- Social media and entertainment
- Addictions
- Domestic violence
- Conflict
- In-laws or families
- Death of loved one
- Illness

I will explain this deeper in chapter 6.

There are even more root causes than listed above, but every problem starts with the self. A husband wants his way, a wife wants her way, and so they war with one another. Then they find it hard to listen to each other, because both jump up onto one another, trying to win. Many excuses get in the way of solving the problem.

Every moment of your life, you will be tempted to move unwisely for your personal gain or personal attention. Temptation will attack the desires of your body and your soul to pull down your spirit.

The book of James clearly talks about where temptation comes from, he said: "What is causing the quarrels and fights among you? Don't they come from the evil desires at war within you? You want what you don't have, so you scheme and kill to get it. You are jealous of what others have, but you can't get it, so you fight and wage war to take it away from them. Yet you don't have what you want because you don't ask God for it. And even when you ask, you don't get it because your motives are all wrong—you want only what will give you pleasure" (James 4:1–3 NLT). Until both partners practice selflessness, they both will fight the battle to prove their own self-righteousness, which is full of heaviness and darkness.

I came from a different country than my husband. We both have our own way of understanding words, actions, and behaviors. It is so easy to misunderstand each other; it doesn't take much to make one angry. Because of our different characters and natures, misunderstandings happen between us. We both are used to certain ways of being. When different approaches or explanations are involved, both of us feel disrespected or dishonored. It was a constant battle until we learned how to be selfless at the feet of Jesus. Before we did that, we didn't know and couldn't understand each other.

There are so many ways that misunderstanding happen. You can look back on any story from your past and see how all misunderstandings happen. Even after knowing Christ, you can see how the flesh, which is the body and soul's desire, can jump up easily. A lot of couples fight with one another about little things, such as different choices, ideas, and wants. You already know a small fire can burn down the whole house. It is good to always be humble, be truthful, and ask forgiveness when you are wrong. Proverbs says, "A gentle answer turns away wrath, but a harsh word stirs up anger" (Proverbs 15:1 KJV). You lose nothing by being humble or apologizing to others, and instead you gain respect.

Differences Bring Challenges

The differences between men and women are challenging. Men and women have their own strengths and weaknesses and have had their differences since the beginning. When a woman is supportive in one area, a man may not be, but he can be supportive in another area. One may be patient, and the other may not. One may talk more, and the other may not. It is good to see, understand, and balance life for both, as everything can change.

Men see in a unique way, as do women, and sometimes both see differently. However, if both can share, discuss, and communicate about these differences and be patient with one another, problems will not be too hard to solve. Nothing is impossible when they can agree. It is hard to deal with when both are weak in the same area. It's good sometimes to have differences in different areas, because both can help each other and strengthen one another.

For example, some men don't like shopping, while some women can really shop. They can spend hours upon hours in the store. When a man goes to the market to buy things, he often really knows what he wants. When a woman goes to buy a thing, it is really a thing. She will easily come out carrying several items from the store beyond the original intent. If women go inside to buy household items, they will come out with some unnecessary grocery items. It's true!

Here is another example. A woman asks her husband to help her with a garden design. Presenting her design to him, she tells him what she wants to do. The man will calculate according to what his woman wants. Believe me, from the beginning of his work, the woman will change her mind on the design several times before he even finishes it. This causes him to redo some of the work and can irritate the husband.

Without understanding our different natures, men can constantly complain about women's sensitivity, and women can constantly complain about men's insensitivity.

The natures of men and women are so different in relationships. If both spouses are not standing together firmly on the foundation of humility, they will fight tooth and nail to overcome each other. They both will run away when it comes to dealing with difficulties and challenges. It is easy to operate in the body and soul. This realm is selfish and greedy and brings confusion, problems, and chaos. A small difference can bring irritation between the spouses and cause bigger problems. Due to these added problems, separation tends to happen more frequently. Know that separation will never happen over just one issue!

Check out these differences. Women are more capable of managing multiple tasks flowing simultaneously. Men get irritated when they do several things at the same time, but they are faster at absorbing information, so they are more responsive. Women are more detailed, and men remember more about the important points. If you ask a man, "How are you?" He will reply, "Fine." When you ask a woman, please know that you need several minutes to listen to her details. Women use nearly three times as many words a day as men do. In most cases, men and women do not behave, feel, think, or respond in the same way.

Because of these differences, misunderstandings come. Unresolved, they build up. A buildup of personal differences can cause friction quickly without solution. It happens in little areas, such as not helping with home chores. Arguments can break out easily. Then, they both stop talking to each other because of a lack of communication, which then brings stress. Stress can disturb us personally in the mind and the body. This happens because of our unrealistic expectations of one another. Also, we compare ourselves and each other to other people. People can annoy each other even over a small thing, which can cause irritation and anger. This can bring a lot of stress, to the point of not enjoying intimacy.

Do you know what happens then? Both spouses start giving their attention to other things or people. The relationship goes on hold. More selfishness and greediness creeps into their lives, they start controlling and being controlled by money. Then they both suffer from a lack of support and a lack of concern for one another. Just when it seems bad enough, outside problems start to arise. Continuous problems come, one after another, to the point when they raise their hands and say, "I am done." That is how infidelity can happen easily to any couple if they are not sensitive to one another and to God. They can manipulate each other when they don't stop the problems the moment they begin. Whenever any temptation comes your way, either you should run away from it like Joseph or face it or fight it by the strength of God to overcome it like Jesus.

Issues, Human Mindsets, and the Craftiness of the Enemy

Couples can easily argue and create misunderstandings from nothing. Understand that pointing, sarcasm, and contempt will chip away the foundation of your marriage. This kind of behavior creates a culture of disconnection. If one or both partners are unwilling to be humble or soften the marital conversation and stop fighting, the problems will get worse until there is no coming back. If it happens once, it is not that hard for a couple to forgive, but when it happens over and over, trust is broken. Just a simple wrong response can ruin the entire day, which makes the disconnection a bigger issue for both. Sometimes both parties' opinions and ideas are good, but misunderstandings arise and cause great conflict.

There are so many things Satan can use to break your marriage covenant. He can use the weakness inside of both spouses as well as outsiders. Satan hates covenants. He can't stand them. It irritates him when he hears two people agree to be obedient to one another in God. You know why? When two or more people come together in agreement, the power of God is so strong that Satan can't do anything. That is why Satan, our enemy, always wants people to be separated and left alone; then he can bring them down easily, just as he brought down Adam and Eve in the garden. Because he cannot be forgiven anymore, he lives with eternal damnation. He always had a plan to destroy, and he whispers into people's ears to bring out those plans so that he can blame humankind.

Satan believes that what he did in the garden, he can do again to anyone when the person is alone. This is where Satan tries to convince people to carry out his destructive plans. Same common temptation will overtake you. The mind is our own enemy; it always compromises. The mind can take control, whether good or bad. It can give sickness, cause problems, and cause wickedness that most don't even know about. A small mind can tear down, poison, or kill instantly; on the flipside, it also can bring life abundantly that is filled with love, peace, and joy.

This is the craftiness of the enemy.

When the mindset of humankind was attacked, twisted, and blinded, this caused sin after sin. Then, demonic forces took over and haunted some of our minds. Some cannot help themselves and end up with mental disorders. It seems as if there is no hope for them anymore. In every country, suicides and murders are increasing. Jails are overcrowded, and hatred and anger seems to have no end. Divorce rates are becoming higher and higher, and people's hearts are torn. It seems like more and more sicknesses are coming, medicine intakes are increasing, and people don't know or understand that those medicines block the way of the Holy Spirit. All of this comes together after just a small spark of believing and obeying Satan words when he says, "You can do it by yourself without God; you don't need Him."

Satan is a liar, a father of all lies. We can't do anything without God, for He is our strength, our redeemer, and our provider. He is the Alpha and Omega. He is our hope who overcomes all things, and we can do all things through Him!

The strength to overcome temptations comes from changing your thoughts and letting God move inside of you. Humble yourself, and accept that God's favor might be upon you by opening your heart and mind. Allow Him a place to reign. Then He will give you new ideas, which will remove all your heaviness and darkness and give you a marvelous light.

Living in a country where I had never been before and where I do not have family of my own, I can tell you that it was hard at the beginning, and I felt very alone. Darkness crept in where I felt heavy inside my mind and heart, and I couldn't help myself. Right there in my heart, I knew that the devil was trying to destroy me by using my circumstances. I knew I didn't have strength on my own to fight against the darkness, so I knelt and cried out to Jesus. At the end of my prayer, light was all over me, and darkness fled. With the power of God, I overcome that darkness.

Break the Ice of Misunderstanding: Communication and Sharing

Communication is a road to your destiny. If you don't communicate, you cannot reach your destiny. Through communication, you will also discover many new things. Communication is interesting, exciting, and full of adventure. You already know communication with God helps you in your relationship with Him as well with your spouse. So practice effective communication not only with God but also with your spouse. The more you build up communication, the closer you get to one another and the more you will break the ice of misunderstanding.

Find time to make yourself available to God and your spouse. Give your relationship priority. Through sharing and communication with one another, you both will be able to understand each other better.

Note that there is destructive conversation as well as productive conversation.

Destructive Conversation

Destructive conversation is like "selfish conversation," which brings turmoil, heaviness, and problems. Unfortunately, some of us grow up in homes where we learn that a loud voice and unshakable personality can win the war. Some are good at holding their breath to keep the peace, but the anger inside may not necessarily subside. Eventually it will explode when it is too much for them to carry. Constant battles in these types of conversations can lead to serious destruction for everyone. While others are constant speakers, they may not consider if others are listening attentively or not. Communication is not a debate to see who wins. It is not about having a powerful voice or strong opinion to make someone agree with you. Putting fear in somebody's life by controlling the situation makes the situation worse. Seek the true answer for better living in Christ for you and others.

Productive Conversation

Here are some points on how to communicate effectively:

- ➤ Get comfortable, listen to your heart, learn how to bring out the point. Remember to use a love language that respects who you're talking to, whether the topic is difficult or neutral.
- ➤ Give your partner your full attention, and ask for his or her attention. Turn off or put down any distractions, such as your

phone. Let your body language send a message of connection, especially if you are concerned that the topic may create distance.

➢ Make eye contact and show your confidence. Use *I* instead of *you* to take the pressure off your partner and show your humility. This shows that you respect the other person.

➢ Listen attentively when the other person speaks and try to see his or her point of view. Don't jump to make a point while he or she is speaking; be patient. Discern what the best result is that you both can come up with in truth.

Break the Ice

The greatest distance between two people is misunderstanding. Misunderstandings can happen easily when there is a gap between both of you, so communication is the first tool that a couple can use to break the ice of misunderstanding. You might not feel like communicating, but if you know it's going to help the situation, gather your strength, be interested in one another, and take your time to communicate. Trials and challenges come every day from both sides as well as from outside the marriage. In every situation, try to gain understanding by searching the truth to solve the problem. Proverbs 4 explains it clearly: "Wisdom is the principal thing; therefore get '*wisdom*': and with all thy getting get *understanding*" (emphasis added).

Sometimes the problem is too great to understand, or the problem is actually multiple unsolved issues that have piled up. In such cases, you know you cannot solve it by communication. Slow and steady wins the race. Be patient, handle one issue at a time, seek the Lord, and He will help you as He promises. God says, "I will instruct you and teach you in the way you should go; I will counsel you with my loving eye on you. Do not be like the horse or the mule, which have no understanding but must be controlled by bit and bridle or they will not come to you" (Psalm 32:8–9 NIV).

Even though every relationship has its ups and downs, successful couples have learned how to manage the bumps in their lives and keep their love lives going through God. They learn how to walk through the complex issues of everyday life with fasting and prayer—seeking the Lord. Always remember to give priority to God and then to one another. Communicate, share, and discuss, and then put your hope in God. Effective communication is medicine for a relationship and builds a strong bond within a couple. It uplifts the heart and brings healing to the body and soul.

Blot Out/Crucify the Issues Caused by the Self

No flesh will be justified in God's sight. Therefore, blot out/crucify any issue you caused. You can do this with fasting and prayer. Everyone needs to go through self-sacrifice by crucifying the self and all its work on the cross. People's problems are all the work of self: self-righteousness, self-gain instead of self-sacrifice, or selfish ambitions.

The Bible says, "People who are self-seeking and do not obey the truth, but obey unrighteousness" will receive "indignation and wrath" (Romans 2:8 NKJV). It is very dark to walk away from God and obey unrighteousness. People disobey the voice of God by obeying self-desire, and they want out of their selfish ambitions for self-honor. They look for God's blessings without the sacrifice of obeying God instructions (the Bible), so they do not receive what they ask.

In the Bible, the book of James asks, "Who is wise and understanding among you? Let him show by good conduct that his works are done in the meekness of wisdom. But if you have bitter envy and self-seeking in your hearts, do not boast and lie against the truth. This wisdom does not descend from above, but is earthly, sensual, demonic. For where envy and self-seeking exist, confusion and every evil thing are there" (James 3:13–16 NKJV). Show others in humility and self-sacrifice, not self-seeking behavior.

People find it hard to cry out to God, but Jesus (the perfect example) cried out to the Father,

"who, in the days of His flesh, when He had offered up prayers and supplications, with vehement cries and tears to Him who was able to save Him from death, and was heard because of His godly fear, though He was a Son, yet He learned obedience by the things which He suffered." (Hebrews 5:7-8 NKJV) He set an example for all to follow on how to carry our own crosses. Look at how valuable it is to learn obedience like He did! No one is born perfect. We all need learning.

So, "For if we have been united together in the likeness of His death, certainly we also shall be in the likeness of His resurrection, knowing this, that our old man was crucified with Him, that the body of sin might be done away with, that we should no longer be slaves of sin." (Romans 6:5-6 NKJV)

Divorce and Separation: Tribulations

Understanding the Root Causes: The Secret of Satan

Most problems and issues can be avoided.

We have already mentioned many problems, their root causes, and how to overcome them. There are many more issues in life that causes division, separation, or divorce. It is good to be wise and understand the things of God. How and why do these issues happen?

All things happen for a reason, and when you find out the reason, you will know how to handle and solve the problem with love. Tribulation comes in a married life for many reasons, whether to purge out all the weaknesses in a person or to test his or her faith. Tribulation also can prune a couple to bear more *fruits* in *God*, because challenges in life also strengthen the inside of the spirit when they seek the Lord. If people do not seek the Lord, destruction is not far from them.

Due to a combination of life circumstances, perfect spouses can become hateful or misunderstanding spouses. In so many circumstances, one doesn't get what one expected. There is always a choice: Either gripe, complain, nag, and nitpick until your ideal picture of married life is finally met (which might be never), or turn to the true lover, Jesus Christ, and wait upon Him patiently.

Nothing will kill a marriage faster than two people who are concerned with meeting their own needs and desires. There are many problems and issues in married life, and a lot of them can be avoided, fixed, or resolved. Neglecting one another or breaking trust can be the main problem. Separation or divorce can happen easily between a couple when there is an unresolved problem hiding under the rug. The problems vary from person to person, but most of them are similar. Temptation is common to all men. Many problems can arise in a Christian's home, even though the husband and wife have the same religion. When a couple is not standing together in the same belief, the problems and issues are different from a couple that does. However, some problems are hard, challenging, and cause deep roots of anger and resentment.

How It Happens and What Causes It to Happen: The Secret of Satan

Satan's biggest tool is that he speaks lies, overwhelming people with guilt and shame, and steals our identities from God. Here are seven deadly sins this demon uses to tempts people:

- ➢ Pride (boasting, self-exaltation)
- ➢ Envy (jealousy)
- ➢ Wrath (extreme anger)
- ➢ Sloth (laziness)
- ➢ Greed (loving money, wealth, and power)
- ➢ Gluttony (addictions, greedy or excessive indulgence)
- ➢ Lust (intense longing or craving for power, control, and pleasure, especially sexual desire)

Lust has nothing to do with love. It is often confused with love, but it is purely physical attraction and has no lasting effect. And no flesh shall enter God's kingdom nor stand in the righteousness of God.

Satan is the father of all lies, and he loves to destroy any good relationship. Because he is a destroyer, he is full of jealousy, pride, and anger. He comes to steal godly identities, kill hope, and destroy all blessings. Satan had a great relationship with God before the fall, but he broke it eternally in heaven. Now he can't have it anymore. He is kept in eternal bonds under darkness, awaiting his final judgment on the momentous day. So, with the little time he has, with his anger, he runs hard to destroy the sons and daughters of the kingdom of God on earth.

With his twisting ideas, enticing words, and promises of shortcuts to happiness, he offers people the seven-demonic power written above. He tries to fool people, luring them as he did Jesus. He takes the weaker ones by force, by using human power. He brings the weak into captivity to be tortured and tormented under darkness. He trains them up to live in the dark and brainwash them, so they will not even know how to live under the light anymore. He plans schemes day and night to kill, steal, and destroy as much as he can before his time comes.

Satan knows that when the mind of a person is twisted, it brings disorder and chaos. He loves to attack people's weaknesses and bully and abuse them. Then he puts the blame on them with his accusing words and makes them helpless. He loves to mix up every mind so that the weak will not be able to think straight to know the right way. This is where a person can make wrong decisions, such as ending a relationship unexpectedly. Satan knows his ability to hurt one person can hurt others, such as spouses, children, both sides of the family, relatives, friends, and others who are around them.

The main thing is that it hurts God, who created all. This hurt can further carry on from generation to generation, bringing division caused by anger and a lack of forgiveness. Because of the deep pain everyone goes through, fear rules over victims' hearts. Destruction is easy and can spread fast. Building up to heal those affected areas can take a long time, but the Bible says, "do not fear those who kill the body but cannot kill the soul. But rather fear Him [the living God] who is able to destroy both soul and body in hell" (Matthew 10:28 NKJV). God heal all pain and hurts.

Some situations are not that hard can be easily dealt with using your own strength and what you have learned, seen, or heard. But they can drain you, and when that juice of strength is sucked up, facing another situation can become a nightmare. Satan loves to see when people are out of ideas and solutions. When they are helpless and stand in a place of darkness with anger, he is pleased. That is the very situation Satan uses to destroy lives. Satan is cunning, a twisting serpent. He will twist your mind to destroy your life. He will not take responsibility, much as he didn't with Adam and Eve. In this situation, know that the answer is in everyone's hands, either physically or spiritually. Where will we seek our help?

This is how to overcome yourself by the power of God through His instructions and His wisdom in the Bible:

Wisdom says, "Do not enter the path of the wicked, and do not walk in the way of evil. Avoid it, do not travel on it; Turn away from it and pass on. For they do not sleep unless they have done evil; And their sleep is taken away unless they make someone fall. For they eat the bread of wickedness and drink the wine of violence. The way of the wicked is like darkness; They do not know what makes them stumble. But the path of the just is like the shining sun, that shines ever brighter unto the perfect day. Give attention to the word of God; Incline your ear to what He is sayings. Do not let them depart from your eyes; Keep them in the midst of your heart; For they are life to those who find them, And health to all their flesh. Keep your heart with all diligence, for out of it spring the issues of life. Never say anything that isn't true, get away from deceitful mouth. Have nothing to do with lies and misleading words (put perverse lips far from you). Look straight ahead the path of your feet and let all your ways be established in God. Do not turn to the right or the left; Remove your foot from evil. (Proverbs 4:14–27 NKJV)

Common Problems and Issues in Married Life: How to Handle Them

Common problems and issues in married life are as follows:

- ➤ Jealousy and stress
- ➤ Boredom and lack of communication
- ➤ Being negative: anger and bitterness
- ➤ Family involvement
- ➤ Not being equally yoked
- ➤ Unreasonable expectations
- ➤ Managing finances (controlling)
- ➤ Destroying trust, infidelity

Jealousy and Stress

As you already know, men and women's abilities and personalities are different. A couple can become jealous of each other because of their different abilities, talents, and skills. Just a small situation can change the whole situation, such as one spouse's personality getting more attention than the other spouse. Are you secretly jealous of your spouse's talents and skills? Do you get offended when your spouse receives recognition or an award? How about feeling jealous when your spouse interacts with anyone of the opposite sex? Being overly jealous is not good, because it will become overbearing and can cause your marriage to turn sour. If you have an overly jealous partner, being with and around him or her can become challenging and stressful.

It is good to find the true motive of your spouse's jealousy. God's jealousy is not like the jealousy that men have. God's jealousy comes out of His love. He knows what is best for His children, for He wants to bless everyone with all good things. Some spouses may be overly jealous because of an experience they have had, such as rejection. It is good to find the truth, get healing from God by confessing to one another, and forgive each other. God wants you to live in the present, not the past. If spouses can understand this, the achievement of one person will cause rejoicing in the other.

Stress is a widespread problem in married life—physical, emotional, mental, and spiritual stress. Stress within a relationship can be caused by many different situations and instances, including finance, family, sickness, and illness. Stress can also come from work, the news, the world, church, or other people. I met a lady who loved to research all the hidden news to find out the truth. She was so concerned about what's going on in people's lives or in the world. Whatever she discovered caused her stress, and she couldn't do anything except worry. She didn't realize this; she was so consumed with the news and her stress that she didn't even see the truth. Listening to her stresses me out, so imagine how it is for the people who live with her, such as her family or spouse! Many different things trigger stress, but what matters is how you handle it. How you handle stress can reduce it or make it worse. Many people take medicine due to stress, and medicine has a lot of side effects. So how do you deal with stress?

Humankind can only carry a certain weight of burden. God understands, as it is written, He says, "Come to Me all who weary and burdened, and I will give you rest. Take My yoke upon you and learn from Me, for I am gentle and humble in heart, and you will find rest of your souls. For my yoke is easy and my burden is light" (Matthew 11:28–30

NKJV). It is always good to take a break and find peace in God. How you take care of your stress will also depend on what kind of stress you have.

Deal with physical stress with physical exercise, proper diet, and a good lifestyle. Get rid of all unnecessary things/junk that can weary you or pull you down. For emotional, mental, and spiritual stress, deal with the Lord, seek His help and cry out to Him. The arm of our heavenly Father will receive all your burdens and heaviness. He will comfort, heal, and provide for you according to your needs, just as He promised. He will give rest to your soul and spirit. Make time for God, and never take a long break from your relationship with Him. The Bible says, "For bodily exercise profits a little, but godliness is profitable for all things, having promise of the life that now is and of that which is to come. This is a faithful saying and worthy of all acceptance" (1 Timothy 4:8–9 NKJV).

Boredom and Lack of Communication

Boredom is an underrated but serious marital problem. When you are newly married, you find a lot of things to do, but eventually boredom will strike you. Some spouses become bored with their relationship, and their communications becomes lazier day after day. They may get tired of the things that occur within the relationship, because it has become predictable.

I was once asked an important question before I married my husband: "After marriage, a day will come when you get bored, so what you are going to do?" I thought hard. I knew getting bored in life was easy, whether one was alone or with others. I didn't know a solid answer. Then I sought the Lord. I said, "Lord, what will I do?" The Lord my God, who is full of love, said, "Daily, be in My word and seek Me." My mind and heart lights up with what He said to me. I can feel it deep inside; the joy springs up underneath my heart. He renewed me right there, and since then I haven't wanted to depart from the word of God. He indeed renewed my daily relationship with joy.

In another way, it is exciting to be spontaneous with taking trips, going for rides, taking vacations, seeing movies, going out for dinner, buying gifts, and doing activities together. Keep the spark alive. If a relationship lacks spontaneous activities, there is a good chance for boredom, and this will become a problem. These activities will help release toxins out of the mind and bring a couple closer to each other.

The most important thing is to connect with God. He will renew your heart and mind, which will renew your relationship with your spouse. Also, it is good for a housewife or mother to find things to do at home, such as creating hobbies, setting up fellowships with friends who have the same spirit, or visiting people and reaching out with prayer and encouragement. Reading or writing in a journal are a couple of ideas that can help you enjoy your day. Do not get your entertainment just by sitting in front of the TV or listening to music without doing much. Physical exercise or working around inside and outside of the house is good to remove toxins from the body and mind.

As you give priority to spending time with one another, share about your daily work experiences or the thoughts and ideas you both have. My husband and I share things every day about how our day went and what God revealed to us. It's amazing. The more we share, the more we realize the miracle of God and the more we get closer. Communication and sharing will open the road of understanding toward one another, and you will avoid a lot of problems.

Being Negative: Anger and Bitterness

When each individual starts gripping his or her own opinions and individual attitudes, the harmony of the union will start facing new challenges. Anger and bitterness mainly comes from the absence of understanding, and a wounded heart or soul can carry negative thoughts.

The Bible says, "Where do wars and fights come from among you? Do they not come from your desires for pleasure that war within you?" You want what you don't have, so you scheme and kill to get it. You are jealous of what others have, but you can't get it, so you fight and wage war to take it away from them. Yet you don't have what you want because you don't ask God for it. And even when you ask, you don't get it because your motives are all wrong—you want only what will give you pleasure. (James 4:1–3 NLT)

I understand. It is so easy to push the button for what you like and want. At times humans are too stubborn in holding onto unnecessary things. They hold onto things from the past that can weigh them down easily and, in turn, become sour in their hearts. Then what they have to say may not be too pleasant for others to hear. The tongue is a little member, and no one can tame the tongue. It carries life and death. Mostly negativity comes from a wounded heart, soul or spirit.

Until they humble and heal themselves, their problems will never be solved. They will continue to argue until a major fight happens. The fight is only to prove one's self-righteous acts and to let others know one's superiority. This is pride that brings strife, anger, and resentment. When all of these things come together, the relationship becomes unhealthy and can cause major physical, emotional, mental, and spiritual sickness.

With any issues or problems, it is good to take time out to understand the situation and heal before it turns negative. Do not make a sudden decision while you are angry. Find out God's answer. At times, you can be stubborn yet still humble unto God. Humbleness unto God is also the key to opening the door of wisdom and understanding, because God's grace means more to those who are humble.

Everything happens for a reason, and that reason, when you find it out, will open your eyes further and bring you up to the next level of wisdom and understanding. It will also help you understand what to hold, when to speak, and when to listen. When a person is negative, he or she needs understanding, love and comfort. Address the issue with understanding, love, truth, and respect. By doing this, you are helping turn *incapability* to *capability*.

In my early marriage, one morning God opened my heart to realize how important it is to speak a blessing to my husband before he goes to work. I start blessing him every day by telling him a positive word from God, and I can see my word brings life to him. That life covers and protects him, which is a blessing for me as well as for him. It was amazing to realize that these small but important things in life really matter. I see the glory of God shinning upon us and giving us light.

Family Involvement

Involving family in the problems between you and your spouse can put a huge barrier between the two of you. Parents, brothers, and sisters—even your own children—can bring separation between the two. For instance, a mother or father-in-law who is constantly involved in the life of her or his children might try to tie the couple down with her or his family's values and culture without the couple's consent. Or a spouse may pay more attention to his or her children than to God or the marital relationship.

These kinds of issues will bring such challenges to the couple, and they will be overbearing and stressful. Sometimes, the hardest thing for a loving parent is to let go of his or her children and let them live independently. The word of God says in Mark, "What God has joined together, let no one separate" (Mark 10:9 NIV). The authority is in the hands of the couple. Whatever they allow in their relationship will happen accordingly. There are choices, so choose the decision that is best for the relationship, no matter how hard it may be. Do it for the growth of the marriage. Do not obey just because of family tradition or cultural value; do things according to the word of God, you will go well in life.

If you can allow your parents or any family relatives to guide and encourage you instead of letting them stand in between the two of you, that will be a great support. There is nothing wrong with asking for other ideas from them, but don't let them make the choice for you. Do you love your parents and respect them? If yes, that doesn't mean you are going to let them rule over your relationship, right? You can let them understand by explaining to them with respect. Same with children: don't let them stand in between the two of you. Always give priority to your relationship with your spouse, which is a part of the relationship you have with God.

A couple can face challenges when one spouse is doing things for family or friends without the consent of the other spouse. A mother constantly giving her grownup children what they want without the consent of her husband, for example, can bring a lot of mental and emotional strain into the relationship, which can lead to a separation.

You may be helping friends who are in need financially without letting the spouse know, which can also break trust in the marriage and lead to separation. Before you come across such things, listen to God and respect one another as husband and wife in God. Never let things come in between you; you both have the power in your hands to allow it or to stop it. Like God told Cain, "You will be accepted if you do what is right. But if you refuse to do what is right, then watch out! Sin is crouching at the door, eager to control you. But you must subdue it and be its master."" (Genesis 4:7 NLT) Obey righteousness and truth.

Not Being Equally Yoked

Not being equally yoked certainly happens when a Christian marries a non-believer. If you marry someone who has a different belief, certainly there will be differences and disagreements within the marriage. Such marriage problems are extremely common in cross-cultural marriages.

But here I am discussing couples with the same beliefs. Couples with the same beliefs can also suffer from not being equally yoked with one another in spirit. With time, if a spouse stops growing in his or her spiritual life, he or she can easily fall short and strain his or her spiritual walk.

Also, some spouses associate with non-believers outside their relationship, such as colleagues at work or friends with different beliefs; such non-believers can easily pull down a relationship, and the couple can suffer tremendously. It is always good to share with one another and to seek God and His guidance, for God doesn't want us to consume ourselves with non-believers. Before you uplift the non-believer, he or she will pull you down. As it said, "Do not be misled, bad company corrupts good character" (1 Corinthians 15:33 NIV). It is good to learn to say no to non-believer friends.

When you associate with God-fearing people who have good hearts and minds, this helps you form and develop your future. It doesn't mean you must depend on them; depending on others is not the true answer. It is God you will need, for in Him all things start and end. He makes things beautiful and complete according to His purpose and glory.

Unreasonable Expectations

Expectations are powerful and can set us up to be either content or doomed to our perpetual feelings of dissatisfaction and disappointment. Over time, when unreasonable expectations are not fulfilled, that disappointment can cause major turbulence in a relationship. Learn where these expectations come from and try to avoid them.

Never compare your spouse to another spouse or to other people and then decided your spouse is not meeting your expectation. Everyone is special in his or her own way. Some of the major expectations a couple can have are honesty, respect, love, decent work ethic, helping one another, understanding and agreeing with one another in decision making etc. Most human expectations, however, come from selfishness. Selfish expectations don't do any good for couples; instead, they create confusion. The wife expects her husband to be more loving, and the husband expects his wife to be more respectful. When a wife expects her husband to be a certain way and a husband expects his wife to be a certain way, and those expectations aren't met, unhealthy blame follows.

It is good to discuss such challenges and resolve such matters daily. Never hold onto things with anger that the other spouse may not even know about. Holding anger can become worse, because it can pile up and cause serious destruction. Effective communication resolves a lot of issues and protects from other issues that will come. In the beginning of our marriage, I noticed that my husband and I hardly shared our anger or frustration. I saw that we often kept it to ourselves, which one day I realized was not healthy at all. I decided to make time for both of us to sit down and discuss those issues. We discussed how to communicate and help each other deal with those issues when they happen. In such circumstances, unnecessary expectations intervene that we may never know how to solve. Instead they accumulate frustration and anger. It is really healing to solve issues that spring up in marital life with understanding from God.

The Bible says, "Do not to let your anger control you, don't let the sun go down while you are still angry, for anger gives a foothold to the devil" (Ephesians 4:26–27 NIV). Anger will come along, but don't let it sit there; solve it by sharing and forgiving, and then move on. When anger sits unresolved, it will eventually blow up. People may not show anger because they are controlling themselves. They believe in their strength, thinking they are strong enough to hold on. But unresolved hidden anger is like a disease that kills slowly. Address it, and heal it; don't let the sun go down on it. Submit your anger to God, and seek His help. Anger is not sin, but it is so easy to sin in anger.

Have the perspective of God once you understand things of God. You will come to know that what God wants from the both of you is more important than what either of you individually wants. Both of you are members of His body. A member of Christ's body does all things for Him alone, without any selfish expectations. Work together with love for Him. As the Bible says, "Therefore, whether you eat or drink, or whatever you do, do all to the glory of God" (1 Corinthians 10:31 NKJV).

Managing Finances (Controlling)

Money plays a big part in a relationship. If left unchecked, financial problems can ultimately destroy a married life. It can break the trust and then break the love and the connection. It is sad! Today's world is so corrupt that money rules. Many believe that love can be purchased by money when they seek to fulfill their own fleshly pleasures. God is serious, and when He says things, He means them! He still means them, even in our modern and fast-paced world. The word of God never changes. Listen to and obey Him, for it is for your own good. Couples are meant to be one, and they should operate as one body, one soul, and one spirit, with freedom inside their hearts. Don't leave room for the devil to sneak in, as he will destroy you.

There are common financial problems that can create issues. They are materialism, the conflict of having different accounts, the adoption of traditional roles when they don't fit, having a difference in money handling, or handing out money to others without the consent of the spouse.

A materialistic couple rates at the bottom of the happiness scale. Materialistically minded individuals can easily destroy married life. Materialism is addictive and hard to control, and once a person enters that stage, he or she needs help. Some people think objects will give them happiness, so they buy, spend, and collect more than they need in life. It can become a disorder and bring problems into their lives, opening the door for the devil to enter and mess up their lives.

A materialistic spirit is a depressing spirit. Depression can sneak in unknowingly, and it's hard to get rid of it once it gets through. Materialism is like purchasing a house you can barely afford or about buying unnecessarily expensive things that create a high debt. For the borrower is slave to the lender. Do you think the credit companies care that you are struggling? No, they don't! It's not their problem; it's yours.

Understand this: focusing on accumulating things instead of accumulating a strong marriage will create tension and depression, which will take away peace, joy, and harmony in a relationship. The Bible warns everyone saying, "Watch out! Be on your guard against all kinds of greed; life does not consist in an abundance of possessions" (Luke 12:15 NIV).

How many people think highly of themselves because they get what they want?

Being overly ambitious brings pride. Pride brings strife, because pride is an abomination to God.

Couples may have differences in handing finances. One may be a big spender, while the other one saves. It is good to work together and sacrifice for one another by having the same goal in God. Nothing is too hard when it comes to the fear of the Lord. If you belong to God, so also does your money! Whatever you have belongs to Him. Valuing and honoring what God has given you will give you understanding, and you will know how to use it wisely. God wants you not to think highly of yourself; instead, be humble. He wants you to get wisdom and understanding from Him. He wants you to not conform to the pattern of this world but be transformed by the renewing of your mind. Then you will be able to test what God's will is—his good, pleasing, and perfect will. Honor God in your possessions.

The word *couple* means "two in one." It means not to operate in different directions. Stand together as one. In every direction, be one, whether in finance or family matters. A couple with two different accounts without mutual understanding can lead to separation. They can foolishly spend money, which can cause misunderstanding, which can break down their trust of one another. Do not open the door to dishonesty, for it says in the Bible, "He who is faithful in what is least is faithful also in much; and he who is unjust in what is least is unjust also in much" (Luke 16:10 NKJV).

Destroying Trust, Infidelity

It is easy to destroy trust, but it's hard to build it again. Destroying trust in your marriage mainly comes from cheating, telling lies, and keeping secrets from your spouse. So many wonder why love fades and people in a relationship grow apart; it is one of the great mysteries. What prevents you from maintaining the passion, attraction, admiration, and closeness you once felt for your partner? What makes the couple grow away from its first love? Infidelity is a widespread problem, and it happens in a relationship for so many reasons. Everyone knows it is a sin, but so many can't control themselves.

The Bible says, "But each one is tempted when he is drawn away by his own desires and enticed" (James 1:14 NKJV). Temptation is not a sin; it is a sign of weakness, which is within you. If you can sense any evil desire (lust) in yourself, ask God to help you blot out/crucify that iniquity. It is good to address the issue before it becomes a problem. Speak to someone who can help you and pray for you.

Avoid what can increase your temptation; avoid those people, places, movies, entertainments, and other areas that can pull you away easily. Be like Joseph who ran away from sin rather than stand and face it. The Bible says, "Run from anything that stimulates youthful lusts. Instead, pursue righteous living, faithfulness, love, and peace. Enjoy the companionship of those who call on the Lord with pure hearts" (2 Timothy 2:22 NLT)

Also know that people may not seem the way they look and the way they speak. Enticing words are deceptive. Listen to the Holy Spirit, who will give you discernment, so you will be able to walk away from deception. To paraphrase Proverbs, the lips of the adulterous person drip honey, and her or his speech is smoother than oil; but in the end, she or he is bitter as gall, sharp as a double-edged sword. The adulterous person's feet go down to death; her or his steps lead straight to the grave (Proverbs 5:3–5 NIV).

The most common sin a person commits is sexual sin. This sin goes straight to destroying a soul, and Satan knows the weakness of men and women. He entices them by using people, television, the internet etc. Some are truly addicted and can't overcome it with their own strength. These people commit adultery with their eyes, and their desire for sin is never satisfied. They lure unstable people into sin and become well trained in greed. Then they live under God's curse. It's sad: so many unstable people are weak inside and out. Seductive spirits will arouse your feeling, but pure love will uplift your spirit. Be wise, and don't fall for a short enjoyment that is followed by a bitter ending. Instead, see what's going to come, and step away from it as far as you can.

Even God understands how painful it is when a relationship is messed up. His heart was broken to see Adam and Eve commit adultery with Satan (by obeying Satan). He was sad to see that both sold themselves out to Satan because of a lack of understanding. Thereafter, God's relationship with them was broken, and God divorced both.

Proverbs 6:32–33 says, "But whoso committeth adultery with a woman lacketh *understanding*: he that doeth it destroyeth his own soul. A wound and dishonour shall he get; and his reproach shall not be wiped away" (KJV, emphasis added). You know how terrible it will be to face God with your unfaithfulness? Without the blood of Jesus, nothing can make the unfaithful clean again, and if they don't accept that, they will not be spared in the day of vengeance.

Don't take for granted what you have. A spouse may not necessarily realize how special his or her relationship is until it is lost. That is why, without knowing it, some tear their relationships apart, sell them out, or abuse them. When they realize, it may be too late. Every relationship is important in the eyes of God.

God loves to have a good relationship with everyone. He is calling everyone daily, whether you want it or not. God wants to bless everyone to live in harmony, free from burden, with joyful marriages and successful lives for His glory. Psalm says, "Blessed is the one who does not walk in step with the wicked or stand in the way that sinners take or sit in the company of mockers, but whose delight is in the law of the Lord, and who meditates on His law day and night." (Psalm 1:1-2 NIV)

According to the Bible, "Marriage is about union, about being joined or bound together to fulfill the promises of God. So, I say, walk by the Spirit, and you will not gratify the desires of the flesh" (Galatians 5:16 NIV).

7

The Reward of the Faithful: The Crown

The Miracle of Those Who Walk in Faith Faithfully from Darkness to Light

Walk by faith in the midst of the storm. Transforming miracles happen when faith is activated in God. Faith is counted as righteousness, and all the promises of God are based on faith.

"Now faith is the substance of things hoped for, the evidence of things not seen." (Hebrew 11:1 NKJV) That substance is of Christ Jesus, His Spirit, and the evidence of things is all His promises that are invisible to our physical eyes. In Him and Him alone do we trust. Faith is a very important tool; it's like fuel for strength. With faith, you believe in what you cannot see, and you do so without a doubt. Faith is like a ship that carries you to the glory realm of God where you will find hidden treasure. Humankind received the Holy Spirit by faith, and our inner spirits are activated through faith in God.

Faith can be operated in every situation. Faith can fail you when it is operated in the wrong way. Everyone in this world was given a measure of faith from God. Whether they operate it or not, they still were given faith. Some have faith to get the wrong things in this world, and their prayers are not answered. Some faith is dead because of inaction on the believer's part. As is said in James, "What doth it profits, my brethren, though a man say he hath faith, and have not works? can faith save him? Even so faith, if it hath not works, is dead, being alone" (James 2:14, 17 KJV).

The Bible also says, "So, then faith cometh by hearing, and hearing by the word of God" (Romans 10:17 KJV). And in Matthew, it is written the power of faith, "The power of faith is, if you have faith as a grain of mustard seed, you shall say unto this mountain, remove hence to yonder place; and it shall remove; and nothing shall be impossible unto you" (Matthew 17:10 NIV). A *mountain* means obstacles, challenges, struggles, hardships, and other difficulties. Faith is powerful, active, and put it into action without any doubt. You can do all things through Christ Jesus.

My mom, despite her abusive and heavily drinking husband, put her faith in God and continued praying for him with tears in her eyes for many years. I've seen her praying for my father and their children more than five times a day. I've seen her tears and heard her prayers. She may not have been the strongest or the most spiritual mother, but she was a wonderful example of a helper.

God was really strengthening her in her journey, and He blessed her tremendously. Her blessing will not stop, because she raised me, a woman of God who continues in her footsteps of praying for others. God uses me tremendously to touch people's lives with healing and restoration, building them up in the spiritual realm. In the year 2000, four years before my dad passed away, he received Christ and became born again. These were the best years of my family's life.

During those two years, mother created, through the love of Christ, the best memories. If she was divorced back during the worst of times, she may not have seen those joyous years. We may not have had happy memories. My dad may not have been saved. Her faithfulness, love, efforts, determination, hope, prayer, and belief really paid a great price. Because Jesus Christ sacrificed, many are saved, and through Christ, when another person sacrifices, many more will be saved. The Bible says, "Those things, which ye have both learned, and received, and heard, and seen in me, do: and the God of peace shall be with you" (Philippians 4:8–9 KJV).

Remove and overcome all self-obstacles by fasting and prayer. Self-obstacles are examples of unbelief and self-doubt. Self-doubt can happen by looking at the problems that are in front of you instead of foreseeing the power of what the Spirit can do. So, allow the power of God to work in you by faith, and let the Holy Spirit manifest in you so that your faith will lift higher and higher. You will see wonder upon wonders, miracle upon miracles. It is not by your strength or the strength of the world but by the power of the Spirit living inside of you that mighty work will happen.

Wait on God Patiently by Trusting Him Completely

Living under the shadow of darkness is unfamiliar territory. I didn't know what to do; it was frustrating. One thing I remembered was that I prayed continuously and asked God to show me the answer. Being newly married and living in a country totally new to me, I was really feeling alone and too far from my family, friends, and people I knew from back home. It was tough to live a normal, happy life. People don't know how my life was. I battled every day for three to four years. Thank God for my sweet husband, who loves me and stands beside me through thick and thin. During the time of my battles, tears were my daily food. I got attacked left to right in my soul, body, and spirit, but I didn't give up seeking the Lord and praying.

Later I realized that God allowed me into this place for a reason, and I can see now that God wants me to totally trust in Him, not depending on my family, friends, or acquaintances. I thank God for allowing me to go through those processes. He cleansed me inside and out, developed me, and blotted out my soul's ties that blocked my way to Him. Now I can hear Him as clear as a bell. I can hear Him anytime, anywhere, and I have a better understanding of Him. He transformed me from darkness into light and brought me into His glory.

Married life is not an easy road, as it's full of responsibility, challenges, bumps, ups, and downs. It is easy to get caught in our human nature's desire to rule over situations and circumstances with anger and frustration. It may not be fair when you look at what you are facing from one stage to another. This is where the blame game can start. You can stand in a stage of complaining and frustration and can make your own decisions and be done with it. But know that this is not the answer. Our human decisions run away from the problem, just to face another problem.

Satan used my situation to hurt me and wanted me to live in frustration and anger. He wanted me to be negative to myself and to my husband, using many circumstances to destroy our marriage. Satan is cunning and sneaky. He silently attacked me behind my back through people, circumstances, and situations. Sometimes he used people to hurt me with crafty words—he especially used my own family, people whom I count on. Through them, he traumatized and abused me, treated me like dirt, and later abandoned me with hatred. But Satan didn't win. The victory is in my hand, and I know these people are not bad because they hurt me. It is because of Satan who blinded them; he took advantage of my weaknesses to hurt me, to bring me down, and to try to break my covenant. I stand facing those hardships with my faith in God, and God rewards me beyond measure. He gives strength to my weak bones, strength to my feeble knees and gives me wisdom and understanding to overcome all things. We know that "we are not fighting against human beings but against the wicked spiritual forces in the heavenly world, the rulers, authorities, and cosmic powers of this dark age" (Ephesians 6:12 GNB).

Overcome Darkness to Light

It is hard to understand what is happening in life, especially when you face one problem after another, seemingly without end. There are times when you can't even explain the situation, because the issues you face are so personal. Facing a controlling spirit, for example, is not easy. This worldly spirit is very strong, very sensitive, and very protective; you can't just fight and get over it. If you are trying to change someone or keep someone away from the problem, you may not succeed. Controlling your spouse from accessing his or her controlling nature can become a weakness for both of you. Be careful not to multiply the problems, and know that you are not the answer. You can't solve it by yourselves. If you do, it will be a temporary fix.

Difficulties and challenges are dark areas in our lives. I've seen so many couples consulting counselor after counselors to get answers for their questions about what happened in their married lives. The most common problems, we already highlighted. Problems may not always be the same, but any problems that come along the way are dark and cruel.

When you stand in the middle of problems, it is hard to find the right people able or willing to help you spiritually. When I stood in my most difficult moment, when I couldn't even figure out what was wrong, I looked around for people who could help me. It hurts, because there was nobody I could rely on to comfort me deep inside. During those periods, my husband and I were new to spiritual ways. We both struggled a lot inside and out. We were weak and could not just comfort each other as we wanted, plus we were newly married. Everything was new to me: people, places, the language, behaviors, and local nature. It was lonely, and I felt like I was in jail. I was frustrated and angry at others and myself most of the time. Every day was a battle, not only for me but also for my husband. I was on the ground daily, laying down all my complaints to God with tears and groaning inside. My husband also was seeking the Lord. God led us and wanted us to solely rely on Him, because He is the answer for every situation and circumstance.

If you face similar things in your life, one thing I can assure you of is that people in the Bible faced the same things. No one could help them with what they needed internally, but they held onto the faith they had in God. Look at Abraham, who walked alone with His family. No one could help him spiritually; even his wife couldn't help him. But God fulfills every need, and He is the only one. Joseph walked alone, but God was with him and fulfilled his needs. David understood so much when he wrote, "Even if I walk through the valley of the shadow of death I will not fear no evil; for You are with me; Your rod and Your staff they comfort me" (Psalm 23). Seeking complete comfort in spouses will not fill you. Yes, they can comfort according to what you need, but the true comforter comes from the Holy Spirit.

During our difficult moments, God comforted us, provided for us, and revealed things to us beyond our imaginations. We both are overwhelmed by the wisdom, glory, power, and understanding that He gave us. We see miracles, signs, and wonders every day. In fact, He wanted us to rely on nobody other than Him because He has much greater things in store for us. He wants to bless us, and He couldn't bless us with the junk we were carrying before. That is why He allowed us to go through those tribulations so that He could cleanse and sanctify and create us anew in Him. Now He gives us complete transformation from darkness to light.

The Bible says, "The righteous cry, and the Lord hears and delivers them out of all their troubles. The Lord is near to the brokenhearted and saves those who are crushed in spirit. Many are the afflictions of the righteous, But the Lord delivers him out of them all" (Psalm 34:17–19).

God developed my husband and me so much that now we help others who are broken and "become the voice of the voiceless to give freedom to those who are captive."

When God transforms your heart with love and understanding, you will see many miracles, signs, and wonders. As the Bible says, "For our small affliction, which is but for a moment, is working for us a far more exceeding and eternal weight of glory, while we do not look at the things which are seen, but at the things which are not seen. For the things which are seen are temporary, but the things which are not seen are eternal" (2 Corinthians 4:17–18).

The Incredible Reward of the Faithful on Earth and in Heaven: Eternal Glory

For the eyes of the Lord run to and fro throughout the whole earth, to shew Himself strong in the behalf of them whose heart is perfect/loyal toward Him.

—2 Chronicles 16:9 (KJV)

There are three stages of transition: the body, the soul, and the spirit. Don't be amazed; you will face a lot in this transition period that you may not understand, but hold onto God. What you see now is like a dim image in a mirror, but you will see Him face to face in Spirit. What you know now is only partial, but you shall know Him completely.

Marrying a person on earth is an example of the moment when you accepted Christ in your life; you are His bride. Jesus doesn't just want a bride; He wants a bride walking with Him in Spirit and in truth. As he says in the book of John, "Anyone who wants to serve Me must follow Me, because My servants must be where I am. And the Father will honor anyone who serves Me" (John 12:26 NLT).

Sometimes you learn a lot of things from the Bible, but without a practical walk, you will not be able to understand fully the meaning. It's important to ask God in truth and honesty. God loves to share, loves to reveal, and loves to talk, because it brings joy to Him when He sees people who walk with Him and listen to the truth. As He says, "My people will worship Me in Spirit and in truth." If you embrace truth, you will hate all lies, and the Holy Spirit, who is the spirit of truth, will guide you in truth all the way of your life.

Let the glorious richness of God strengthen you with power through his Spirit in your inner being so that Christ may dwell in your heart. Be rooted and established in love, which has power, and know that this love surpasses knowledge—that you may be filled to the measure of all the fullness of God. He can do immeasurably more than all you ask or imagine, according to His power at work within you.

Be blameless, pure, and sanctified; this is the will of God. Obey God in sanctification of your body, soul, and spirit, and you will live under the liberty of what God has freely given you: His kingdom on earth. The complete blessing of God is incomparable to anything else; have a peaceful mind, knowing that what we have cannot be purchased by the world's richness.

Obey the voice of God, even as hard as it can get. Be separated for Him, and do not touch unclean and detestable things. Be the perfect lamb, a pleasing aroma, and an acceptable sacrifice to God. By your obedience and sanctification, you fulfill the law of love. Jesus said, "He who has My commandments and keeps them, it is he who loves Me. And he who loves Me will be loved by My Father, and I will love him and manifest Myself to him. We will come to him and make Our home [dwell] with him" (John 14:21 NKJV).

When God the Father, God the Son, and God the Holy Spirit dwell in you, you become the tabernacle of God on earth. You become the Oracle of God for His people. For the Spirit will reveal to you all the hidden things from the Spiritual realm supernaturally. Having God's heart, seeing how God sees, and hearing how God hears is a blessing. It's not the perspective that comes from you or the church or denomination or pastors or leaders or prophets or anyone on earth. It's God's perspective that will be revealed to you, for the ways of men are before the eyes of the Lord, and He ponders all His paths. He judges all things accordingly and will bless you abundantly on earth and in heaven; you will live with God in eternal glory wherever you are.

Enjoy your eternal inheritance on earth or in heaven, which you received because of your sacrifice by faith in God. You will lack nothing from Him.

As is written in Proverbs,

"Incline thine ear unto wisdom and apply thine heart to understanding; criest after knowledge, and liftest up thy vice for understanding; seekest her as silver, and searchest for her as for hidden treasures; Then shalt thou understand the fear of the Lord, and find the knowledge of God. For the Lord giveth wisdom: out of his mouth cometh knowledge and understanding. He layeth up sound wisdom for the righteous: he is a buckler to them that walk uprightly. He keepeth the paths of judgment, and preserveth the way of his saints. Then shalt thou understand righteousness, and judgment, and equity; yea, every good path. When wisdom entereth into thine heart, and knowledge is pleasant unto thy soul; Discretion shall preserve thee, understanding shall keep thee." (Proverbs 2:2–11 KJV)

THANK YOU

GOD BLESS YOU ALL

Printed in the United States
By Bookmasters